# My Life Is Not My Own

# My Life Is Not My Own

Dr. Crystal A. Champion

MOUNTAIN ARBOR
   **PRESS**
Alpharetta, GA

The author has tried to recreate events, locations, and conversations from her memories of them. The author has made every effort to give credit to the source of any images, quotes, or other material contained within and obtain permissions when feasible.

Copyright © 2022 by Crystal A. Champion

All rights reserved. No part of this book may be reproduced or transmitted in any form or by any means, electronic or mechanical, including photocopying, recording, or any information storage and retrieval system, without permission in writing from the author.

ISBN: 978-1-6653-0202-9 - Paperback
eISBN: 978-1-6653-0203-6 - ePub

These ISBNs are the property of Mountain Arbor Press for the express purpose of sales and distribution of this title. The content of this book is the property of the copyright holder only. Mountain Arbor Press does not hold any ownership of the content of this book and is not liable in any way for the materials contained within. The views and opinions expressed in this book are the property of the Author/Copyright holder, and do not necessarily reflect those of Mountain Arbor Press.

Library of Congress Control Number:  2022902586      0 3 0 1 2 2

∞This paper meets the requirements of ANSI/NISO Z39.48-1992 (Permanence of Paper)

Author Photos by Theresa D. Photography, Ayesha Lakes of PhoArtgraphy, LLC

*I dedicate this book to all people who are actively fighting cancer, cancer survivors, and those who have lost their battle with cancer. I am inspired by your courage, your will, and your strength. I also want to dedicate this book to anyone who has lost a loved one who has helped shape them and helped them to find their purpose in life. Lastly, I dedicate this to my family, who has always supported me and encouraged me no matter what and has always has motivated me to reach my fullest potential. I would also like to thank the people that crossed my path, who taught me life lessons, whether they realized it or not.*

———

*I also dedicate this book to purpose-driven people, people who feel that they should be doing more but don't know how to get there, and people who have had life-changing experiences and don't know how to use them to help others.*

*"The two most important days in life are the day you are born and the day you find out why."*
—Mark Twain

# Contents

*Preface*
*xiii*

*Introduction*
*xv*

**Phase One: Life Lessons in Childhood, Family, and Career**

Chapter 1: Humble Beginnings
3

Chapter 2: School "Daze"
13

Chapter 3: The Seed Being Planted
25

Chapter 4: Missed Opportunity
27

Chapter 5: Broken Confidence Served with a Side of Shattered Ego
29

Chapter 6: A Path Diverted
35

Chapter 7: Growing Pains
41

**Phase Two: Life Lessons in Trauma, Tragedy, Faith, Spirituality, and Love**

Chapter 8: Early Trauma
47

Chapter 9: Tragedy Versus Faith (Round One)
55

Chapter 10: Tragedy Versus Faith (Round Two)
63

Chapter 11: Seasonal Yet Purposeful People
69

Chapter 12: Developing Patience Through My Patients
87

Chapter 13: Illogical Logic
101

Chapter 14: Accolades, Applause, and a Pause
105

Chapter 15: Trial and Transition (Vision 2020)
119

Chapter 16: First Quarter 2020
—Consciousness and Confirmation
125

Chapter 17: Showtime or No Time
137

Chapter 18: The Shake-Up and the Wake-Up
145

Chapter 19: The Aftermath
151

Chapter 20: Pandemic or Peace?
155

Chapter 21: Pre-Existing or Just Existing?
165

Chapter 22: Second Quarter 2020—Coming Out
177

Chapter 23: Protests and Prosperity
183

Chapter 24: Third Quarter 2020—Taking the "Ls"
191

Chapter 25: Vision 2020—Year-in-Review
197

**Phase Three: Life Lessons
in Finding My Purpose**

Chapter 26: Purpose Defined
205

Chapter 27: Lightworking and Energy
211

Chapter 28: Confirmation and Inner Promptings of the Spirit
217

Chapter 29: My Inspirational Influence on Others
221

Chapter 30: The Point and Purpose of It All
227

*Gallery*
233

*Bibliography*
239

# Preface

THIS BOOK IS IN NO WAY INTENDED TO IMPOSE UPON the readers my religious beliefs, views, or opinions; however, I am merely sharing how my spirituality has played a part in finding my ultimate purpose in life. I have often been questioned about being so young and already knowing my purpose in life. "How did you arrive at this point?" people ask. "How do you truly know this is your purpose? How do you know this is your purpose and not just something you are good at?" I am not a religious leader, and I am certainly no expert on the human race. I am, however, well versed on my life and the experiences that have shaped me, and I can only share with you the promptings I have received and continue to receive from my inner voice and intuition, which I also equate with the Holy Spirit.

I look at it this way: When my life has come to an end, what legacy will I leave behind? What will I be remembered for?

> "What we have done for ourselves alone dies with us; what we have done for others and the world remains and is immortal."
>
> —Albert Pike

I have always known that I was destined for something much larger than myself or, at times, something way beyond what my mind could even fathom. I want to be known as someone who selflessly touched the lives of everyone she encountered and imprinted upon them her stamp of positive influence. In the words of First Lady Michelle Obama, "We've got a responsibility to live up to the legacy of those who came before us by doing all that we can to help those who come after us."

I feel that finding your purpose requires deep self-reflection, thorough self-knowledge, self-awareness, meditation, and whatever avenues and principles you use to guide your life. If you are not aware of yourself, how can you be of service and positively impact the lives of others in the way that you intend?

My memoirs are just that, a collection of events and personal experiences that have led to self-reflection, self-knowledge, and self-discovery of my moral compass. I pride myself on being a private person. I have often been told that I am difficult to read, difficult to figure out, and that I am an "intriguingly complex" individual. With that being said, I expose all of my vulnerabilities in this book in the hope of enlightening someone else through my failures, my moments of brokenness and sadness, as well as my moments of happiness and successes.

Ask yourself this question as you read this book, "How can I add value to the life of someone else?" I hope that you find inspiration in my life lessons. I bid love, light, blessings, and purpose to all who are reading.

# Introduction

DECEMBER 31, 2019, A DAY THAT I WILL NEVER FORGET. It was a day in which I received news that would change my life forever. I was in a complete state of denial, shock, and disbelief as I sat in my car in a parking lot. I was in a twilight zone, a space that I had never experienced before in my life. I couldn't even allow tears to roll down my face. How could this be happening to me? Why did life have to throw me such a curveball right now? All the hard work I had put into my business and nonprofit was finally starting to pay off, and now my life would have to come to a screeching halt. Lord, why this timing? Why this date? Why on New Year's Eve? Now I will be forced to face this horrible memory every year! Lord, what was I being prepared for? Your word says You will never put more on me than I can bear, but the uncertainty and gravity of this heavy moment are too much for me! I knew people looked at me as such a strong, resilient soul, but *come on!* I have helped many others through this same situation, yet I didn't have the words to comfort and encourage myself. Certainly, this could not be how my 2020 was going to start. I am a good person. I have a heart for serving and helping others. What was the purpose of me going through this? Please make it all make sense!

# Phase One
## Life Lessons in Childhood, Family, and Career

# 1

## Humble Beginnings

SEPTEMBER 23, 1981: I WAS BORN INTO A STRONG-KNIT Christian family in the little rural town of White Plains, Georgia, a town with a population of only 293 people and no traffic lights—just a caution light. It's so small that if you drive through and blink, you'll miss it! Traffic and life in general were and still are slow. Nobody is ever in a hurry and everybody is related or knows everybody else. Pretty much everybody is your "cousin." Often you'd get stuck driving behind a slow-moving tractor carrying hay or have to stop in the middle of the road to allow the cows to cross to the other side of the pasture. The nearest grocery store and the schools (elementary, middle, and high) were at least a fifteen-minute drive from where we lived. The nearest shopping malls, movie theaters, and other forms of entertainment were at least an hour's drive away. White Plains is known for Holcomb's Barbecue. The food is so good you have to get up early in the morning just to get those fresh pork skins with hot sauce! If you waited until after noon, you were out of luck. My family was so country that my dad owned cows and chickens. He also had two beagles, a male and a female, that he rabbit hunted with all the time. Dad would clean up the rabbits good, and my mom would cut them up, fry them, smother them in onion gravy, and make rice and fresh, homemade buttermilk biscuits on the side. Talking about some good eating!

The dogs would always chase the chickens around the house between two to three a.m. and my dad would roll out of bed and fire his rifle outside to stop the madness! My dad also loved to garden and still does today! He would grow everything such as collard greens, cabbage, tomatoes, corn, butter beans, peas, cucumbers, and hot peppers. He even tried his hand at strawberries, watermelon, and muscadines. We also had a peach tree in our yard. Dad would always make the best homemade peach preserves. My sisters and I would toast white bread and make peach preserve sandwiches. That's just how good it was!

In the summertime, we frequently turned on the TV or popped a tape into the VCR and watched something we had recorded and sat in the den and shelled bunches of peas and butter beans. Our thumbs used to hurt so bad by the time we were done! We didn't have anything else to do in the country, so may as well shell peas! We never had cable and we had an antenna that would often get stuck. My dad would go outside to turn the antenna to make sure it was unstuck and we would yell out of the window, "Whoa!" whenever the TV picture was finally clear. It was a treat to go to my grandmother's house to watch TV once she finally got one of those huge satellite dishes! Being able to watch music videos on BET was a luxury!

The road we lived on was a dirt road for a long time. It was first paved with gravel rocks, then blacktop several years later. I remember my parent's cars, a 1987 four-door sedan and my dad's baby blue 1950-something pick-up truck always kicking up dust coming down the road.

I am the youngest of three girls. My sisters are thirteen months apart and are six and seven years older than me. Everybody used to think they were twins because they always dressed alike and wore their hair the same. Then I came along. I really believe I was unplanned. I always joke with my parents and say, "I was an 'oops,' but the best oops ever!" My sisters and I were all very close. Even now they still treat me like I am the baby of the family. I used to feel so left out when they would go to the store or hang with their friends and would tell me, "You are too little to go." When they were in school and I wasn't, the highlight of my day would be seeing the school bus stop in front of the house to let them off. I always ran outside to greet them. They often brought me snacks from the snack machine at school. My favorites were the barbecue corn chips and white cheddar popcorn. One day I got so excited that my sisters were coming home from school that I pulled up my dress and mooned the bus, panties showing and all. My sisters were so embarrassed and still constantly remind me of that moment!

I spent a lot of summers in Atlanta, Decatur, Georgia—in Dekalb County to be exact. I couldn't wait for summer breaks from school so I could spend time with my cousins. Growing up in the country, there wasn't much to do. In Atlanta, I could go to the mall and the movies. I could swim, skate, and play with my cousins and have fun making play-dough pies and cooking with the baking oven specially made for kids. Speaking of swimming, one of my aunts always let us go swimming at her community swimming pool, which was called ECA. One summer, me, my sisters and cousins went to the pool. We were all in the water, standing around, and somebody jumped in the pool, making a large wave that knocked me under the water. I almost drowned. I don't remember who pulled me up out of the water, but I was very young and didn't know how to swim. I became absolutely terrified of water from that experience!

On a lighter note, one of my other aunts always took us to Sgt. Singers Pizza Circus on Memorial Drive, which was pretty much the old-school version of modern-day pizza entertainment restaurants. I would be so excited watching those characters on stage singing and playing their instruments.

I was always excited to see my favorite uncle. He was the

cameraman of the family. Every family gathering, he had his video camera to capture every moment. My sisters, cousins, and I loved for him to visit, especially when he traveled from Atlanta to visit White Plains. He brought the sweetest and best cantaloupes and watermelons for us. The yellow-meat watermelons were our favorite! I loved watching him stand outside, slicing cantaloupe and scraping the seeds out of the middle. He sliced up the melons with the rinds still on and handed them to us. We had all kinds of juice running down our faces and clothes, but it was the best!

We looked forward to family reunions and family gatherings. We had a large family that gathered for every major holiday. We celebrated our church anniversary and homecoming in August on the second Sunday of the month. The men hung out all day Saturday and Saturday night before homecoming, making a fire pit out of cement bricks to barbecue a hog. My sisters and I were so excited for all of my aunts, uncles, and cousins from Atlanta to visit on holidays. During these visits, they went to church with us. One of my aunts was a seamstress, so for Easter and Mother's Day she made some of our clothes. I will never forget one Mother's Day, we all decided to wear red and white. Auntie made dresses for her sisters and all the girls out of this red and white polka dot and floral material. We thought we were making a statement that Sunday!

One of my older cousins often babysat me and gave me the nickname "Cookie." Eventually, my nickname got cut short and people started calling me "Cook." It stuck. My family still calls me by that nickname today!

My mother served as the church treasurer and my dad served as chairman of the deacon board at my hometown church, Second Baptist Church. I grew up in the church. I accepted Jesus Christ as my Lord and Savior when I was six, along with my best friend, and we were baptized together. It was Valentine's Day, which happened to fall on a Sunday. I went to Sunday school, church, and looked forward to Vacation Bible School in the summer. I loved hopping on the back of my dad's pick-up truck, along with cousins and other kids in the neighborhood, hitching a ride to VBS. The wind blowing our hair and the sun kissing our skin was like heaven. The best part of VBS was making the crafts and those mixed bags of chips and cookies, washed down with a side of punch. To top it all off, Friday night was hot dog night!

I also sang in the choir and was a youth usher. I was a bit shy but still led a song or two when asked. I used to get so nervous! There was nothing to do for entertainment in the country town of White Plains, so going to church, choir practice, revival, and church trips were our entertainment. We had so many fond memories that involved the church. Sunday dinner after church was a tradition. We frequently had the pastor and his family over for dinner. Oftentimes they were like a second family to us.

My mom worked as a telephone operator, often working weekends and holidays and enduring a one-hour commute to work each way, every day. At the end of her workday, she would tell my sisters and me how much her hands and wrists hurt as she developed carpal tunnel syndrome. As early as the age of five, my mom asked me to massage her hands and feet and would say to me, "Child, you have some healing hands. Those little hands feel so good." My sisters decided to test me out and said the same things: "You have magic hands." At the time, I didn't know that those words would ultimately lead me to find my God-given purpose. When I was born, my dad said he knew I was going to be special from the look in my eyes.

"She has bright eyes," he said. "That means she is going to be smart!"

I have a lot of fond childhood memories of my great aunt, one of my favorite people. She babysat me while my parents worked and while my older sisters were in school. She used to look forward to the first day of every month and referred to it as "check day." She received food stamps and assistance from the federal government. She threw on her best wig, carried her big purse on her forearm, and took her food stamps along with me to the store to buy whatever I wanted. She pushed the buggy and let me put whatever I wanted in it. She kept a deep freezer at her house full of stuff just for me, like frozen pizzas, hotdogs with cheese in the middle, freezer pops, and push-up pops.

My maternal grandmother also kept me sometimes and gave my family the government foods she received that she did not want, such as powdered milk, huge blocks of "government cheese," and that peanut butter in the gray can with black writing on the front. By the way, my mom made the best peanut butter cookies with that peanut butter!

I can remember my great aunt's house did not have a bathroom. We used a metal pot on the back porch to use the bathroom and we boiled our bathwater on the stove. We literally had a "pot to piss in." I often watched her wash her clothes on a "washboard" and hang them out to dry on the clothesline. She and my grandmother also sat out on the porch and churned their own lye soap.

Long story short, my great aunt spoiled me rotten. I always attributed my weight during the majority of my childhood to her feeding me anything I wanted. She gave the best back rubs. I pretended my back was itching just so she could lay me across her lap, pull out her bottle of green rubbing alcohol, and rub my back with her magical hands. She used to always pat me on my thigh and call me her "fat gal." Yes, I was a chubby one when I was little. I loved to sit in her lap and play with the loose skin on the back of her arm, especially her left arm where she had a mole that I was fascinated with.

She loved her cigarettes and beer. I remember one day I kept asking her to try her cigarette and she gave it to me. I took one puff and almost choked to death. I realized she gave it to me to teach me not to develop the habit that she had. She was fearless. I will never forget the day when we were standing in her front yard and she was talking to her nephew across the yard through the pomegranate bushes that divided them. I spotted the largest snake I'd ever seen in my life. I screamed and said, "Auntie, it's a snake!" It looked like it was twenty-five feet long. She found a brick in the yard, threw it with all of her strength at the snake, and killed it! Then she went to the back porch, got a garden hoe, scooped up the snake, carried it out to the back yard, and tossed it into the woods. She walked back into the house like nothing ever happened.

My great aunt never got married and never had children. She

treated my sisters and me like we were her children. If I had the opportunity to ask her one more question, I would ask her why she remained single. I've asked several family members and nobody knows why. Maybe something traumatic happened to her, or maybe she saw the dysfunction of other people's marriages and relationships, or maybe she was just such a strong woman who wanted to hold her own, no matter what it took.

My dad did not finish high school and worked as a grocery store stock clerk and in my old high school cafeteria unloading trucks and washing dishes. He finally retired from working at the age of sixty-eight. I remember he worked at the grocery store during the day and then studied to obtain his high school diploma at night. An older gentleman, who we viewed as a grandfather, was visiting our home one day. He asked my dad a question and asked him to read something and my oldest sister said, "He doesn't know what it says because he can't read." That was all the motivation my dad needed to go back to school. He did it! And even as a little girl, I was so proud of him.

As I stated earlier, Mom was a telephone operator for thirty years. Until this day, I look back in awe at how she worked a full-time job, commuted to and from work two hours each day, managed to cook Sunday dinner-type meals for us every day, did our school shopping, washed and straightened our hair in the kitchen with a hot comb, made sure we were in church, Sunday school every Sunday, and revival and vacation bible school each summer, all without even flinching. She was and still is a tough woman.

My dad was very well known and respected in the community because everyone knew him from working in the grocery store and the school. Because of that, it was easy for my dad to help me find a job. I started working at sixteen and throughout high school and college I was a grocery store cashier at the same store my dad worked at. In college, I came home on the weekends and continued to work my job to avoid being a broke college student, although many times it was hard to even scrape up five dollars to get into the campus parties to dance and have a little fun. I loved being a cashier. I made up in my mind that I would be the best darn cashier ever because I always strived to be the best at whatever I set out to do. Even though it was a humble job, my dad told me to be thankful, be the best, and hold that job with integrity. I learned impeccable customer service skills, interpersonal skills, and time management, which at the time I had no idea would prepare me for my current career as a physical therapist. My work ethic was developed.

My parents taught me the value of hard work, consistency, integrity, and self-respect. They raised me to not get caught up in the hype of materialistic things. I didn't grow up with a lot of things. There was hardly brand-name anything in my house. I wore knock-off sneakers. I also wore hand-me-downs from my older sisters, even their old brand-name shoes that they bought with their own money. The shoes were severely worn out but I managed to clean them up and make them work. Those old shoes were fire by the time I got through patching them up! We barely even had brand-name groceries in the house. Everything was generic. It was a special treat to get the cereal we wanted. It was a big deal to have fancy butterfly entertainment crackers and cheese balls for our birthdays. The ice cream of choice was always store brand Neapolitan or vanilla. Other sweets in the house consisted of the sugar-dusted Christmas tree cookies or butter round cookies and apple sauce. Ironically, my dad pretty much did all of the grocery shopping. He worked in the grocery store so it was easy for him to do the shopping to save my mom from having to do it.

I always felt that my mom and dad had a unique relationship. They have been married for fifty years. My mom worked during the day and some weekends. My dad worked at night. It always seemed like once mom got home, it was time for dad to leave. We always had a parent at home. My mom made more money than my dad, but I never knew it to cause a problem. My mom managed the money and bills for the home, but I would always hear her and dad discussing finances and ways to go about doing certain things. I can count the number of times on one hand that I remember them having a huge argument about anything.

My mom was the disciplinarian of the house. My sisters and I were more afraid of my mom than my dad! My dad was as cool as the other side of the pillow but would still let you know who was in charge. He was and still is very even-tempered and mild-mannered. I always said he wouldn't hurt a fly. However, boys were scared to date me and my sisters or even come to our house because they knew my dad and had a lot of respect for him. I never got a spanking. I was a good child. I learned what not to do to get in trouble by watching my sisters get disciplined. When they got in trouble, I went and hid in the living room in the corner by the front door. I didn't want any part of it! Both of my parents are angels on earth and as sweet as pie. They will give you their last if they had to and many people often turn to them for help and advice.

I am truly blessed to have been raised by Christian parents who went above and beyond to make sure my sisters and I had everything we needed. We never got arrested, used drugs, or got pregnant while in school. We all three have master's degrees or higher. This was definitely an accomplishment seeing as how my parents did not go to college.

I have such wonderful childhood memories with my family. Even now I reminisce about those times of no stress, no pressure, and no worries. When I go back home to visit White Plains, I feel very grounded. The country air, the trees blowing in the wind, the sounds of nature, and no traffic or other hustle and bustle create an environment of peace for me. I have no regrets being raised in a small country town. My upbringing has allowed me to remain humble, focused, thankful, and grateful for the simple things in life.

## 2

## School "Daze"

I WAS A SHY GIRL AND A BIT SELF-CONSCIOUS throughout my school-age years. Considering that I was a girl, I never liked the fact that I had overly hairy arms and legs and long sideburns. Since kindergarten I was picked on in school. I was chubby and heavyset. I would get called Miss Piggy. My sisters used to call me Petunia, who was Porky Pig's girlfriend. It made me cry every time. Even in sixth grade, I vividly remember a boy in my class telling me that I look like I eat at a buffet all the time. I was always the tallest girl in my classes throughout elementary school. The boys I had crushes on would always be way shorter and way skinnier than I was. I didn't stand a chance. In middle school it wasn't much of an issue because the boys began to hit their growth spurts and were becoming taller than me. I was five foot seven inches when I got to seventh grade. I can only remember having a boyfriend in middle school, but even then it was only for a few months. He played football and I was in marching band, playing the clarinet. It just didn't work out. However, I was smart, and nobody could take that away from me! I received the highest GPA award for both my seventh and eighth grade class. In high school, I never really dated. I stayed focused. Along with being in marching and concert band, I was in Beta Club, was the president of the school government, and earned valedictorian for the Class of 2000. Plus, I was so afraid of disappointing my parents by getting into trouble or getting pregnant that it was easier to just fly solo and not date.

I used to be terrified of driving. I watched all of my close friends get their driver's licenses in high school. I still rode the bus to school, even through my senior year in high school. I don't know why I had such a fear of driving. My dad taught me how to drive in his old red pickup truck. My poor dad. I almost gave him a heart attack several times. He used to fuss at me and say, "Stop looking at the nose of the truck and look ahead at the lines in the road!" Needless to say, I tore his nerves all to pieces. I did not get a driver's license until I was eighteen. Not being able to drive was one of the reasons I did not go to my high school senior prom. All of my friends were driving, and I had to rely on my sister to drop me off or, yet again, bum a ride with a friend. It was easier just not to go. Plus, I felt fat and did not like any of the dresses I tried on. I didn't get my first car until my sophomore year in college and I didn't get a cell phone until I was almost a senior in college. I always had to bum a ride with other people. I hated it. I was so independent, and having to rely on someone else was the worst. I am still like that present day.

I went to college at Georgia College & State University in Milledgeville, Georgia. My sisters had attended Georgia College and had good things to say about the school and the academic programs. My middle sister graduated with her bachelor's degree in biology with a minor in chemistry and my oldest sister received her master's degree in special education. My first choice for college was Mercer University in Macon, but even with a partial scholarship being offered, it was too expensive. Other schools sent me college packets in the mail, and one I remember vividly was Johnson C. Smith University in Charlotte, North Carolina. It is an

HBCU, but, again, out-of-state tuition was too expensive. Besides, my parents were not keen on me going out of state for school. Georgia College had a good reputation and was more affordable and it was only forty-five minutes from home.

My best friend since middle school was my roommate throughout college. We had the same major, which was health education with a concentration in exercise science. I was also lucky to get to go to college with another friend I have known since kindergarten.

College was an eye-opening experience. In a way, I felt that my parents sheltered me too much, so some stuff I saw and experienced shocked me. I was still a bit self-conscious and I experienced more insecurities when I got to college. The guys in college seemed to go for the light-skinned girls or those with long hair and big butts. I didn't fit into either of those categories. I encountered girls whose parents gave them credit cards to buy whatever they wanted. I was lucky to have any money left over from my student loans after paying for housing and tuition. Forget shopping and getting my hair done. That just wasn't happening for me at the time. Regardless of these distractions, I remained focused on my studies.

I wanted to be more active on my college campus. Even before I went to college, I was interested in Black sororities and fraternities, also known as the Divine 9, which was also a part of the National Pan-Hellenic Council. I had a lot of exposure to Delta Sigma Theta, being that a lot of my teachers in grade school and my choir director at church were Deltas. They were strong women educators and leaders in the community. I had a lot of respect for them. My oldest sister joined the Iota Psi Omega graduate chapter of Alpha Kappa Alpha Sorority, Inc. in Athens, Georgia. Although she was urging me to become an AKA, I wanted to be a Delta. I attended several events on campus, but I soon learned that some of them had really bad attitudes and I did not want to be a part of that. I shifted my attention to the AKAs. They seemingly ran the campus and their members held several leadership positions on the campus from the Student Government Association to the

Resident Hall assistants to everything else. They were also very friendly whenever you spoke to them. Now that was an organization I wanted to be a part of! There was so much positivity!

When I saw a flyer for an interest meeting for Alpha Kappa Alpha posted in my dorm, Adams Hall, I was ecstatic and went for it! My middle sister gave me the money I needed to complete the process and take care of national dues. Little did I know that at the meeting, the friend I've known since kindergarten was also there! We had never talked with each other about joining AKA but laughed when we saw each other at the meeting. We went through the intake process and officially became members of the Kappa Eta chapter on April 20, 2002. She was my line sister. There were seven sorors on my line and we were called "Ivies of Distinction." I was number five and my line name was Eminence. We bonded as sisters through the process and had some hilarious moments together! I was hoping my roommate and best friend from middle school would join the sorority at the same time I did, but she was not ready and instead joined the following year. We had so much fun participating in step shows, visiting other local colleges to support their Greeks, and, of course, strolling at the Thursday night campus parties. My line sister and childhood friend was eventually our chapter president, and I was vice president. We hosted fun events on campus and our undergraduate chapter advisor was a force to be reckoned with! She kept us in check and made sure we were ladies of dignity at all times.

I thought that joining a sorority would give me a sense of belonging—and it did for a short while—but deep down I still felt like something was missing. I still felt like an outsider. Even though I was a part of this amazing sisterhood, I still felt an emptiness. I felt like I was different from everyone else. Everybody hung out and partied and socialized, and I would often be solo in my dorm room, watching TV or studying.

Georgia College was referred to as a weekend college, because everybody went home for the weekends and returned on Sunday evening. I continued to work at the grocery store on some of the weekends I went home. It was nice to have the extra money.

Whenever I went home, I stopped by on Sunday afternoons to see my maternal grandmother. She was always so happy to see me. Without fail, she would slip me a twenty-dollar bill before I left. She was on a fixed income, so I felt guilty when she tried to give me money. I used to say, "Grandma, I'm doing okay. You don't have to give me anything." Still, she continued to shove the money in my hand and would say, "Baby, take it." She'd give me a glaring look with her beautiful gray eyes as if to dare me to argue. Our visits always ended with a hug and kiss on the cheek. She stood on the porch and watched me drive off and stayed outside until my car was no longer visible. I would toot my horn for one last goodbye.

Initially, my major was going to be biology/pre-med, until I spoke with the head of the exercise science program. He told me that if being a physical therapist was my goal, then an exercise science major was the way to go. In 2004, I graduated with a bachelor of science in health education with a concentration exercise science. I graduated cum laude with a 3.60 GPA.

Even though I had graduated, I still had a summer internship to complete at a physical therapy clinic in Augusta, Georgia. Once that was completed, I immediately went to physical therapy school with only a two-week break for rest in between. I was blessed to be accepted at the school I chose first. My journey at the Medical College of Georgia was about to begin.

To be admitted into the physical therapy program at the Medical College of Georgia, I had to complete an in-person interview with the instructors, complete an essay, and take the GRE. The program was highly competitive and would only accept thirty students for the new semester. MCG required at least a combined score of 1000 on the GRE. I hate standardized tests! I scored a 960 and did not want to take the GRE again. MCG had a "provisional admission" status in place which meant I could be admitted on provisional status under the condition that I maintained a 3.5 GPA the first semester to be granted full admission. I thought to myself, I am disciplined and a fast learner, so I don't think that will be a problem. I went with it. To my surprise, my first semester of physical therapy school was more or less a review of *everything*

I had already learned during two years of my undergraduate major courses. Lo and behold, I earned a 3.8 GPA for the first semester and was granted full admission.

My classmates were like family. We bonded so quickly because we worked in groups, studied together, and had to complete assignments together. Unfortunately, we lost a few classmates from the program due to their GPAs. It was unfair that you could have a cumulative 3.0 GPA but still get dismissed from the program if you failed *one* test and the opportunity for a retest.

My most vivid memory of PT school was my human anatomy class. I took it over six weeks in the dead heat of summer. I also took the class with occupational therapy students and physician assistant students. We had to work on cadavers in the lab. Oh my gosh! "As long as I don't see a face, I will be okay," I repeatedly said to myself over and over again. Luckily, the cadavers' faces remained covered and left for the dental students.

On the first day of cadaver lab, we were split into groups of four to five. Every group had its own cadaver to work on. We were first assigned to dissect the muscles of the upper back to expose the latissimus muscles and other muscles surrounding the scapula and thoracic spine. Our cadaver was male. He was tall with a solid, athletic build. Our first task was to flip the cadaver over onto its stomach so we could expose the back. It was definitely a sight to see my group trying to flip over this huge rigid body with genitals and everything exposed! We were given instructions and the instructor showed us where to make the first incision with our scalpels. After receiving instructions, everybody in my group looked around at each other and swallowed hard. After nobody moved or said anything, I grabbed my scalpel and said, "I'll make the first cut!" My group members looked at me like I was crazy. In my head, I was thinking that if we all stand here like zombies we are never going to get out of this lab and away from the smell of this formaldehyde! I am a woman of my word, so I made the first incision. Once I opened up the skin to expose the muscles, the other group members became fascinated and were more at ease about continuing.

On another day in lab, our assignment was to dissect the hand. It took hours to cut back the skin of the hand to expose the intrinsic muscles, bones, tendons, and ligaments. After what felt like two to three hours of standing and cutting away at the hand and inhaling the scent of the formaldehyde, I became lightheaded and dizzy. I felt like I was going to pass out. I excused myself and rushed from the lab into the hallway where the air was cooler. I sat down on the floor with my back against the wall and tried to take deep breaths. I had broken into a cold sweat. One of my group members came to check on me and brought me some water. After about ten to fifteen minutes, I felt better and went back into the lab to continue. It was at this moment that I realized I had a whole new level of respect for surgeons. Opening up bodies and standing over them for hours on end is definitely not my cup of tea, and anyone who can do that is the real MVP!

The anatomy tests were hard. We had to learn every muscle, every bone, and every ligament in the body in a six-week timeframe. Not only did we have to take written tests in the classroom, but we also had to take tests in the cadaver lab. With the bodies that we had dissected lying on the table, the professor stuck little numbered flags on certain nerves, ligaments, bones, and muscles. We had to correctly identify the structure that was marked. As the final week of class came to a close, the cadavers began to dry out and stink so badly! I will never forget that horrible stench!

As my journey through physical therapy school continued, the classes became harder and harder. During my last semester, just before I was about to go on my last clinical rotation before graduation, I completed my Neurological Conditions class. The instructor was excellent, but the class was hard! We learned how to treat various neurological conditions, including multiple sclerosis, traumatic brain injuries, strokes, and spinal cord injuries. At the end of the class, we took a practicum exam. My case study consisted of teaching a patient with a C5-C6 spinal cord injury how to transfer from a wheelchair to a mat table. I partnered with a classmate who played the patient, and the course instructors evaluated me. To assist with the evaluation, a physical therapist that worked at the local VA hospital came to help. Once my case was done, my classmate said, "Crystal, I know you passed. You did an excellent job!" Once he left the room, the instructors and the new evaluator gave me constructive feedback on my performance. The new evaluator said, "You missed a very important safety step."

I thought as hard as I could, but could not think of one thing that I did wrong.

Finally, she said, "You didn't put shoes on the patient. If you verbalized it to me I would have passed you and you would have had a 96. However, this counts as a safety fail with no exceptions."

My heart dropped to the bottom of my stomach. I said, "Oh, of course I would have put his shoes on."

She chimed in again, "But you didn't verbalize it, so it's a fail."

I had studied and practiced so hard for this practicum and I knew I nailed it. You mean to tell me this therapist, who wasn't even one of my instructors, had the audacity to fail me for one simple thing? I left the room feeling defeated and upset. I thought I was going to throw up. I needed to pass this practicum so I could complete my next clinical rotation to graduate. I went into another room where some of my other classmates were. They all said, "How did it go? I know you passed!" I shook my head no. Everyone's mouths dropped, especially my classmate that played my patient.

He said, "Crystal, you did exactly everything right. What happened?"

When I explained I had a safety fail, they all gasped in disbelief. Sad to say, there were at least ten other classmates who did not pass. The instructors offered us a chance for "remediation," which involved attending study sessions with one of the course instructors and having to repeat the practicum exam. I was super stressed because on the day of my remediation exam, I had to finish moving out of my dorm room. By the grace of God, I passed my practicum exam. I went on to complete my last clinical rotation and graduated in 2006 with my master's degree in physical therapy with a 3.9 GPA.

The next challenge was having to pass my National Physical Therapy Board Exam and the Georgia jurisprudence exam. I had to pass both to receive my physical therapy license. I had already been on several job interviews in Augusta, Atlanta, and Columbus, Georgia. My heart was set on moving to Atlanta and I wanted to work in outpatient orthopedics.

The guy I was dating at the time was on active duty in the army and he was stationed at Fort Benning in Columbus. (At that point, we had been together for three years and I was in love. I will disclose details about this relationship later concerning how it helped shape me into the woman I am today.) I applied for a job in Columbus to be closer to my boyfriend at a prestigious orthopedic clinic. I was excited. I had tons of questions, but after asking the clinic director one question, the interview went south. I asked the director how he felt about continuing education and if the clinic would support further education because I was interested in earning my doctor of physical therapy degree. The clinic had a good reputation for offering excellent continuing education opportunities.

He said, "You don't need to worry about getting a doctorate. It won't do you any good."

Really! Did he just say that to me? I can't lie; I was pissed. He put a really bad taste in my mouth. How dare he try to quench my fire to obtain the highest accomplishment in my career. Aside from that, the interview went really well, and after two days, I received a call back that the clinic wanted to hire me. I politely declined the offer. No, thank you. That clinic was not a good fit for me. The supervisor's comment was the nail in the coffin. I didn't want to work for anyone who would limit my educational growth.

I went on five interviews after graduating physical therapy school: three hospitals and two outpatient clinics. One clinic was in the town in which I went to physical therapy school. Upon leaving that interview, I encountered three other of my PT school classmates who were applying for the same job. Man! Tough competition. I was not chosen for the job.

I accepted a job in Norcross, Georgia, at an outpatient orthopedic clinic that was contingent on passing my exams. The clinic manager was so nice and even said, "If something happens and you don't pass your exams, we can let you work as a rehab tech here until you pass." That amount of generosity made me even more eager to work there. Ugh! Here we go again! First, being fully admitted to PT school was dependent on a standardized exam. Now, another standardized test was standing in my way.

AFTER GRADUATION, I linked up with one of my close friends from PT school who was also my best study buddy. We studied together for an entire month before taking our exam. Starbucks could have charged us rent as much as we went there to study for hours and days on end! My study buddy wanted to move to North Carolina and practice PT there, so she was not required to take a jurisprudence exam for that state. Georgia requires PTs to pass the ethics and jurisprudence exam, which was based on the state practice act and PT laws.

One day as I was sitting in Starbucks, studying with textbooks, notebooks, and flash cards spread out all over the table, I became extremely overwhelmed and exhausted. I don't take standardized tests very well. They always give me severe anxiety. I sat at the table with my head in my hands. I had a headache. I was scheduled to take the exams in two weeks. A young Black gentleman walked past my table, looked back at me, then doubled back to my table. He introduced himself and told me that he was a minister. He proceeded to say, "God would not let me leave this place without giving you a message." He must have noticed the befuddled look on my face, and he quickly continued, "You will pass your exam on the first try. You will also move to Atlanta. When you get there, at some point you will meet a successful businessman. You will have times where you may feel alone, but you won't be."

I looked back at him wide-eyed. How did he know I was going to move to Atlanta? I thanked him for the message and looked at it as confirmation that all would be well.

I took several practice exams online and also bought an exam study book for further preparation. I refused to let that test defeat me. I did take my jurisprudence exam and passed it on the first try. I received the results immediately. Whew! Step one was done. My study buddy and I took the physical therapy licensure exam on the same day at the same time at the end of January 2007. We both walked out of the testing center like two zombies. Our brains were fried. Just for making it through the exam, we treated ourselves to dinner at one of our favorite seafood restaurants. Something about those cheddar bay biscuits soothed my soul. We sat and chatted about the most difficult questions on the exam that we could remember.

"How did you feel about the exam?" I asked her.

"I really don't know if I passed or not. I kept second-guessing myself the entire time," she said.

I told her I felt the same. The results were not available immediately and we had to wait a few days, checking the state licensure website to see if our names were posted to indicate that we passed the exam. Two days had passed and my study buddy called me. She was very ecstatic and was squealing over the phone, "I passed! I passed! I passed!" I was extremely happy for her, but I hadn't yet seen my name posted on the Georgia licensure site which left a heavy feeling in the pit of my stomach. I checked the website over and over again. I can't even count how many times I logged onto that site. I doubted myself and became depressed. I was living with my oldest sister at the time. I kept myself closed up in my bedroom with the lights off, blinds closed, nightshirt on, hair scarf on, and in bed most of those days. Two days after my friend called me with the good news, I sat up, logged into my laptop, and checked the website once more. To my surprise, my name had been posted! I passed on the first try! I ran into the living room screaming and shouting at my sis, "I passed, sis! I passed!" We both jumped for joy. I felt like a huge burden had been lifted. The next day I called the clinic supervisor to tell her I passed my exam. She was so happy for me! A couple of weeks later, I moved out of my sister's apartment and moved to Atlanta! One of my cousins, who lived in the Atlanta area, had an extra bedroom and agreed to let me live with her until I figured out where exactly I wanted to live. I had a long commute daily from Lithonia to Norcross, but I did it proudly. All of my hard work had paid off. I had secured a job and achieved my goal of becoming a physical therapist. I was well on my way! While working full-time for the orthopedic clinic for a year, I completed my doctor of physical therapy degree from the Medical College of Georgia in 2008, earning a 3.92 GPA.

I had finally become Dr. Crystal Champion.

# 3

## The Seed Being Planted

I OFTEN GET ASKED BY PEOPLE I MEET AND MY PATIENTS, "How did you become interested in physical therapy?" I will share with you the same story I tell them. When I was a little girl, I always knew I wanted to be in the medical field. I used to tell my immediate family I wanted to be a dermatologist. I heard the fancy word somewhere, not truly knowing what a dermatologist was. But what I did know, was that it was a career in the medical field. My family would prompt me and say, "just be a doctor if you want to be in the medical field."

When I was in seventh grade, my maternal grandmother, who was in her seventies at the time, had to undergo bilateral total knee replacement surgery. She worked hard as a housekeeper in the local county hospital. All those years of being on her feet, walking, standing, and cleaning on those hard floors had taken a toll on her knee joints. She developed terrible degenerative arthritis in both of her knees. I remember countless number of times watching her struggle to try to stand up from a chair or recliner and it would often take her at least a good ten minutes to be able to come to a full standing position. As she sought medical treatment for her arthritis, one of her favorite doctors told her, "ma'am, both of your tires are flat!" in reference to the fact that both of her knees were severely damaged. I would laugh whenever my grandmother told this story and so would she! Her primary care doctor referred her to an orthopedic surgeon, and subsequently my grandmother endured her bilateral total knee replacement surgery. My grandma was an extremely strong woman. She told the surgeon, "If I am going to do this, you better do both knees at the same time because I am only gonna do this once!" That was her story and she stuck to it. After her surgery, I observed the physical therapists trying to get her out of bed to walk for the first time using a walker. I have treated patients who had knee replacement surgery for one knee and it was very painful and difficult. I often think, "how in the world did my grandma endure all that pain at her age?" She got her tires fixed and once she was discharged from the hospital, I would go to her house to watch the physical therapist work with her. My grandmother would say "baby you need to watch what this therapist is doing because this is what you want to be doing."

As I went through high school, knowing I wanted to be in the medical field, I took a series of health occupation classes that focused on medical careers. My teacher for the class was a nurse by trade. In those classes, my peers and I would rotate through different departments in the hospital to gain more exposure to medical careers, such as pharmacy, respiratory, radiology, nursing, and so on and so forth. I was even trained on how to be a certified nursing assistant. One day, I finally got to rotate through the physical therapy department. On that day, I witnessed a male PT teaching an older male how to walk in parallel bars on his new prosthetic leg. I thought, "Wow, how amazing is it to be able to help someone walk and get their life back!" This was a defining moment for me that really helped me to focus on the path to be a physical therapist.

4

## Missed Opportunity

CONSIDERING I GRADUATED AS THE VALEDICTORIAN of my high school class, you'd think I would have had scholarship offers left and right, right? Not! My school was located in a small district. The only scholarship I ever remember applying for was the Gates Millennium Scholarship which I did not receive. I cannot recall the high school counselors pushing me and others in my class, particularly the "top ten," to apply for scholarships. Because of my GPA, I did receive the Governor's Scholarship and the HOPE Scholarship, but these only covered a portion of my tuition and I had to maintain at least a 3.2 GPA or higher upon entering college to continue to receive these. Needless to say, I had to take out student loans to support myself through college, from undergrad to grad school and through my post-graduate studies. By the time it was all said and done, I had over $70,000 in student loan debt.

In 2011, I dated a very smart guy. He was business-oriented and ambitious when it came to achieving his goals and dreams.

Actually, he was so ambitious to the point that he chose ambition over our relationship. He wined and dined me at the best restaurants and we were always at the local professional parties. His job required him to travel frequently, so at times I would fly out to meet him to squeeze in a getaway. But it turned out he was way too busy to be attentive to my love language (quality time) and we didn't work out. But I digress.

Interestingly, he also graduated valedictorian of his high school class. We once had a conversation about college scholarships. He told me that he went to college on a full scholarship. He was so puzzled by the fact that I graduated valedictorian and didn't receive a full scholarship. As I thought about it, I became angry. I was angry at the fact that I went to a small school, in a county that did not push its students to excel and reach their full potential. I felt that I was on my own. My ambition and my drive got me to where I am today, not a school system that failed to encourage students to go after anything and everything they wanted. Why do people who work so hard to be where they are get the short end of the stick?

Instead of really being able to save money and enjoy the fruits of my hard work as a physical therapist, I was stuck with a monthly student loan payment that was equivalent to a car payment. I applied for a public service loan forgiveness program, in which if I worked for underserved populations and made 120 consecutive student loan payments, the rest of the balance would be forgiven. Well, there was a catch. I had to change from a standard repayment plan to an income-based repayment plan. Switching to the income-based repayment meant that my monthly payments would be almost one-third higher than under the standard repayment plan. That equated to more than half of my mortgage payment! Here we go again. I can't win for losing. Everything has a catch. The middle-class working citizens are truly stuck in the middle. I took one step forward only to have to take two steps back. It's a perpetual cycle.

# 5

## Broken Confidence Served with a Side of Shattered Ego

I THOUGHT I WAS EXCELLING IN MY CAREER AS A physical therapist. Within a year of working at the clinic, I received a clinical excellence award. One of my patients wrote a letter to the company, which was seen by the regional manager, singing me praises about how I helped improve her quality of life. This brought me back to that moment in high school when I saw a PT helping a patient learn how to walk on a prosthetic leg. I thought to myself, so this is how it feels to make a difference, to improve someone's quality of life. That was the most fulfilling feeling I've ever had in my life. All of my hard academic studies finally started paying off.

The small clinic was a part of a larger corporation; however, our clinic was not meeting its budget. Since I was the "baby" of the clinic, the regional manager wanted me to split my time between my home clinic and another clinic about thirty minutes away from where I lived. I really had no say in the matter because I had no seniority.

I floated around to several clinics for about a month and I absolutely hated it. In one particular clinic, the clinic director was like Victor Newman from *The Young and the Restless*. It was his way or the highway. He was very intimidating. All of the employees were tense around him and no one seemed happy. I didn't want to be there. I told the regional manager that I would not be happy staying at that clinic. He looked around for me and decided to permanently move me to another clinic location, one he felt would be a better fit. As much as I didn't want to—and as much as I don't like and fear change—I was willing to make the move because I truly did enjoy working for the company and my benefits were excellent.

I was given the opportunity to visit the new clinic, and I could tell I would like being there. As I started at my new clinic, the clinic director seemed genuinely nice. I was the only Black therapist working there, the same as at my other location, so it didn't bother me. I thought this would be the opportunity for me to stand out and develop my skills as a PT. As they say, however, when in Rome, do as the Romans do. The clinic director had her own way of doing things and seemed to force others working in the clinic to do things her way. That did not sit well with me. I wanted the freedom to develop my own style of treatment. I was doing her clinic a favor by transferring there and helping out because they were getting busy and I was helping to alleviate some of her caseload. Most of the patients in the clinic were long-time patients or repeat patients, so they did not want to see a new therapist. They were accustomed to working with my clinic director and would request to see her instead of me. It became hard for me to meet productivity quotas and it looked as if my job performance was suffering.

I was also at the clinic at the time President Obama was elected. There were employees and patients at the clinic who were obvious racists by the comments they made. One lady said, "If he does get elected, somebody is gonna kill him."

An employee stated, "He's not my president."

Another employee said to me after President Obama was elected, "Well, hun, you must be proud."

I stated, "Everyone should be proud. This is a historical moment for our country."

I was often questioned about my credentials and my physical therapy training. Whenever I said, "I am a doctor of physical therapy," I got the side-eye and blank stares from patients at that clinic. "Yes, I am a Black woman with a doctor of physical therapy degree. Get over it!" was the response I really wanted to make. I was angry, but I needed my job and I had to bite my tongue. Little did my director know, I was in the process of searching for another job. I had even called out sick several times to go on job interviews. Before I had a chance to plan my exit, I got called into a meeting by the regional director and the clinic director. They told me that multiple patients had complaints about me and were requesting to see another therapist. The clinic director even had the nerve to say to me, "I have worked too hard to build up this clinic for someone else to come in and ruin it." They were firing me. I felt blindsided, especially coming from my regional director who had personally given me the clinical excellence award just a few months prior. I was at a loss for words. Being a woman of integrity, I could have just walked out, but I sucked it up and finished the rest of the week. They did pay out the vacation time I had accrued, but being fired and not having another job lined up immediately, I found myself in the unemployment office. I was so embarrassed and hurt. I felt betrayed and like a complete failure. I held my head down in shame walking through the doors of the unemployment office. How did I end up here? I was a doctor of physical therapy and suddenly I had nothing to show for it!

I was fired. Yes, FIRED! The word resonated in my head over and over again. I felt like I did my best at that clinic and my efforts weren't good enough. I wasn't good enough. How was I going to be able to tell my family? I worked so hard to please them and make them proud. What would my friends and associates say and think? I cried for days. How could I be in this position? How could this happen to me? My last name is Champion. I don't fail. I have a DPT, graduated high school valedictorian, and graduated cum laude when receiving my bachelor's degree. How could I be fired from the same company that I received a clinical excellence award from only a few months earlier? My confidence was completely broken, my ego shattered to pieces. Day after day I questioned my abilities as a PT. Still to this day, I shy away from outpatient orthopedic physical therapy due to my horrible experience at that clinic. But this too shall pass . . .

My reason for termination on the unemployment papers read, "Employee failed to meet company standards." What a bunch of tomfoolery. That offended me even more. I went to the employment office once a week to check in, and every week I had to have evidence of applying to at least five jobs. I was able to receive unemployment benefits and with the cash payout I received from my PTO benefits, by the grace of God, I was able to pay all of my bills on time. Lord knows I did not want to be a burden to my family and ask for money. My family was very supportive of me. My mom, dad, and sisters all said, "Girl, you will be fine. You are in the right field so you won't have trouble finding another job." I wished I could have believed them, but at the time nothing was offering me comfort. The time I was not working I used to reflect on myself and to exercise, rest, and go to Bible study. I tried to figure out my next steps. After about a month of being unemployed and frantically applying for countless jobs, I began receiving calls for job interviews. I would get dressed up, confident, and spiffy with my resume in a leather portfolio that highlighted all my awards, accomplishments, employee performance reviews—the whole nine. I felt well prepared for my interviews until I was asked that one dreaded question: "Why did you leave your last place of employment?" I had to be honest. It was documented on file, and if any employer wanted to see it they could. I had to tell the truth and say, "I was terminated." I quickly tried to explain my side of the story and said that I felt that I was not given a fair chance to truly develop my skills as a therapist and that the environment was not ideal for me as a recent graduate PT. Saying you were fired or terminated never goes over well in an interview, and I got the dreaded "Sorry, ma'am, because of that we don't think you are a good fit for our company."

I cried for days. All these interviews and I could not find another job. I even contemplated suing the company for wrongful termination, but I just couldn't bring myself to do it. I began to panic. I was desperate to find any job in physical therapy. I refused to go back to being a grocery store cashier just to make ends meet. That was not on my agenda. About two weeks later, I was hired by a home health agency. I didn't want to do home health, but, hey, they hired me and offered excellent benefits. I started orientation and about halfway through my orientation week, regret set in. I thought, I really don't want to do this job. I went home and began my job search again. I found a position for a thirty-two-hour-per-week physical therapy position (which for that organization was still considered full-time) at a hospital that was seven miles from my home and had only been open for two years. I had never heard of this facility and realized it was a part of a large hospital system in the Atlanta area. I applied for the job, then got called for an interview within two days. It was a small community hospital and the staff I met were all very nice. Once again I got asked the dreaded question: "So, why did you leave your last place of employment?" Uh oh. Here I was again. I knew if I answered the question honestly, they would probably not hire me. I am an honest person and I worry about any little thing catching up to me and backfiring. I was honest during the interview. I also went in armed once again with my leather portfolio, spiffed-up resume, pantsuit, and my side of the story about why I felt that my last job was not the best fit for me. I even whipped out my clinical excellence award. Lord, I needed a miracle and a prayer. I left the interview feeling nervous because I really wanted that job. It was in an acute care setting and the facility was absolutely beautiful. It looked like a hotel, *and* it was so close to my house compared to the thirty- to forty-five-minute commute to the awful clinic I was fired from. Being that it was a small hospital, it was not too intimidating and felt like a great place for a fresh start. I still considered myself a recent grad with only two years of experience.

The next day, I received a call and was offered the job! I was so excited! I notified the home health agency that I would not be working for them, and they told me that I would not be paid for the orientation that I had completed. But I didn't care. I had the opportunity to work for one of the top hospital systems in the South East! I happily signed the job offer. I was beginning a new journey. I realized God closed the door at my previous job so that I could move toward something better, something that I could not yet see. Being fired was not simply a failure. It was a chance for me to rebuild my broken confidence and piece back together my shattered ego.

# 6

## A Path Diverted

AFTER ABOUT A YEAR OF WORKING FOR THE HOSPITAL, I was presented with the opportunity to serve as rehabilitation coordinator for my department. This was a management position but did not have the management title. No one else in my department considered the position. Once people found out that I was being prepped for the position, one colleague in particular made a huge scene about the situation. She said it was not fair that the hospital was not giving other people a chance to apply for or show interest in the position. I asked her, "Well, are you interested in the position?"

"No," she said.

Ha! I thought, then why in the heck are you making such a big deal! I continued to train for the position and perform my duties. It was a huge learning curve when it came to budgeting, conflict resolution between employees, solving patient satisfaction issues, and scheduling, among other things.

After starting the position, I quickly became super stressed. I had a full patient load and managerial duties. I was an hourly employee and was not allowed to do everything needed without going into overtime and overtime wasn't allowed. My plate was full: rehab coordinator, teaching the total joint replacement class, helping develop educational materials, assisting with program development, leading the new employee hospital orientation and volunteer orientation, serving as clinical instructor for PT students, and helping train new PT hires. After an employee transferred, I inherited her role as cancer committee member, a committee I had no interest in serving on. However, no one else stepped up to the plate so I added it to mine. Needless to say, I was burned out. My brain was toast, and I was severely fatigued. I was so stressed that I was drinking two glasses of wine every night. I was spiraling out of control. My family noticed how my attitude and demeanor changed. I was short-tempered with everyone. My sisters and parents said, "This job is not for you. You are doing too much." I didn't even have time to properly care for my precious little four-year-old poodle/bichon puppy named Noah. I had to give him back to my sister, who initially gave him to me when she became too ill to care for him.

I took that position for all the wrong reasons. I thought I needed to prove myself, to show my value and worth. I put my ego aside and resigned from the position after one and a half years. God spoke to me and said, "I need you to focus on your patients." Even after stepping down, I earned the lead PT title. God revealed to me that life wasn't about money or recognition. My job should be a ministry.

After a few years of being at that organization, I began to feel that there was something "more" that I was supposed to be doing. I was becoming burned out *again*. I was the one doing everything in the department but without the title. I did not feel challenged in my career, and I was not growing in my career. I began quietly searching for another job. I came across what I thought at the time was an awesome opportunity at a new clinic, treating people with peripheral neuropathy. I was the sole therapist to help start the clinic. I would learn the new balance equipment and devise all of the documentation procedures. The practice was owned by a chiropractor, and there were two medical assistants, two medical doctors, one physician assistant, and me. It was a chance to start fresh and learn something new. I was super excited. I notified my supervisor at the time that I wanted to work PRN status while I was full-time at my new gig. I wanted to keep that safety net just in case and didn't want to burn any bridges. My request was granted and I started my new job at the neuropathy clinic. As I drove up to the clinic, to my surprise it was right down the street from the orthopedic clinic that fired me. Ha! God, you really do have a funny sense of humor!

I am a person who does not like change. It gives me anxiety. It took me a while to adjust to the new gig. I continued to work PRN at the hospital. After three months, I realized I *hated* the new job. The coworkers were annoying, the doctors were not happy, and it was the same thing over and over every day. I can honestly say that the protocol of the clinic didn't help patients get much better. It was unfulfilling treating a patient and they didn't get better. What really made me hate the job was an encounter I had with an older, white, male patient. I wore my hair natural in an afro at times. As the patient sat in a chair waiting for me to put the electrical stimulation pads on his legs and feet, he stared hard at me and said in the most hillbilly tone of voice, "Girl, what in the world happened to your hair?" He said it loud enough for other people in the clinic to hear. I was a bit taken aback. I was not about to bite my tongue on this one. I snapped back. "It's an afro, haven't you ever seen one before?" He retreated back in his seat and didn't say another word. Everybody else stared at me as if I was going to go into angry-Black-woman mode and start tearing the place up.

The next day, an inner voice spoke to me and said, "Talk to your supervisor at the hospital and see if they have found anyone to fill your full-time spot. You need to go back. Your work there is not done yet." I did just that. My supervisor was surprised that I called and asked the question. I told her that I was willing to come back full time. She delightfully welcomed the idea. Even though I clashed with her in a lot of ways, I learned that I had to put those emotions aside and be obedient to God's plan for my life. God opened the door wide open for me to come back. Several therapists who were interviewed for my full-time spot turned down the position just at the time when I was led by the spirit to swallow my pride. I did not want to face the guilt and shame of what I thought at the time was just another failure. I did not want to face the humiliation of the situation and what all my old coworkers would think. I was in my new job venture for three months. I was required to turn in a thirty-day notice to the neuropathy clinic and I did so immediately. I sighed in relief that I was going back and I told myself that I had to be grateful and have a whole new outlook on being back at the hospital. Just because the grass on the other side looked greener didn't mean it didn't have poop, rocks, and dirt in it!

As I stated earlier, I never fully left the hospital. I remained on staff as a PRN PT. Being that I transitioned to PRN status, I lost my benefits and had to start all over with health benefits qualification as well as earning vacation and sick time but I was okay with that. God quickly revealed to me that I needed to get rid of my ego and pride. Besides, I just couldn't deal with the uncertainty of my new venture. I ignored the red flags because I was into my own feelings and needed to change my environment to prove a point. I was prideful. I felt that I was not appreciated and often thought that they wouldn't be able to succeed without me.

Upon my transition back to full-time, I heard some negative comments. One comment particularly still sticks out in my head. One of my colleagues said sarcastically, "Welcome back! Well, that didn't last long now did it?" Those words were a hard pill to swallow. Nonetheless, I swallowed them straight—no water, no chaser. On the flip side, not only was the transition back a smooth one, but I also came back with less stress and I received more pay! At that moment, I realized that it was not about me and feeling taken advantage of and not appreciated. It was not about my feelings of being tired, burned out, and overwhelmed. It was about greater work that God was preparing me for. My work was only just beginning. Hindsight is 20/20, right? It was a chance for God to show that He was still in charge of my life, my path, and my divine purpose.

Shortly after I returned back to my full-time position at the hospital, my supervisor approached me regarding starting a lymphedema program. My initial line of thinking was, "No, I am not interested. I don't want to limit myself to just doing lymphedema." However, after serving on the Cancer Committee at the hospital, the idea of starting a lymphedema program was brought to my attention again two years later. Cancer treatment services offered at my facility were expanding. My first instinct was again to say, "No, I'm not interested." But my spirit said, "Why not me? You can do this! You have a chance to make a difference and do something *greater*. Isn't this what you have been waiting for?"

I seized the opportunity, and I had confirmation in my spirit that God was nudging my stubborn self in that direction. I took the initiative to do some research regarding lymphedema treatment. I spoke to a lymphedema therapist that worked in my hospital system to find out more about the certification and I shadowed her in the clinic. In less than two hours after the conversation and meeting, she sent me an email—from the same school from which she received her certification—regarding hosting a lymphedema certification program at my facility. "Wow! God you sure do work fast," I thought. I submitted the email to my colleague who was responsible for setting up continuing education opportunities at my facility. Surprisingly, the company was eager to find a facility in the Atlanta area to host the certification course. My colleague requested that my facility be placed at the top of the list as a priority, and we were! So what does all of this mean? It meant that I got to attend a $3,200 course absolutely for free! To make things even better, for every ten participants in the course, my facility received a free space for someone else to get certified. We had twenty-eight participants and another colleague was able to obtain her certification for free. Until it was time for me to attend my certification, I put forth a lot of hard work in researching and continued to consult with lymphedema therapists to get the framework for the program started.

It was a grueling, nine-day certification course, beginning at eight a.m. every morning until seven p.m. each night with a one-hour lunch. All I had time to do was to eat, sleep, and breathe lymphedema. I passed both my written exam and my hands-on skills check with flying colors. Whew, I did it! But, boy, was I exhausted! After I became certified, I spent countless hours developing educational materials and making sure necessary supplies and billing codes were in place until it was time to launch.

The flip side was that the course took place at the exact time as my sorority's national conference, known as Boule. I had never been to Boule and it was also being held in Atlanta! My heart sank when I found out the two events were taking place at the same time. I had to pull out my adult card and listen to what God had placed in my heart: I had to be a certified lymphedema therapist to continue moving toward my purpose! It was no coincidence that both events were at the same time. God made the choice clear, and I am convinced that it was all divinely orchestrated.

Ironically, as I completed my lymphedema certification, I received some sad news. I learned that one of the medical assistants at the neuropathy clinic where I previously worked was diagnosed with stage four cervical cancer. It hit me like a ton of bricks. At the clinic, she used to always complain of low back pain and ask me to stretch her or do manual treatment when we were between clients. No matter what treatment I did, she continued to complain of low back pain. It dawned on me that she had cervical cancer and we didn't even realize it. The low back pain she was experiencing was referred pain from her cancer. Wow! Lord, I wish I had known then and encouraged her to have her back pain checked out a little further! As a result of her surgery, chemotherapy, and radiation treatment, she developed lymphedema in both of her legs. Even when I left the clinic, I still kept in touch with her via social media. She had a seven-year-old daughter. Her sister posted updates on how she was doing. I saw pictures of her in a wheelchair with her legs wrapped in bandages. About a month later, her sister posted that she was in hospice care. About two to three weeks later, she passed away. *Wow, wow, wow.* Even though I took a detour from my path, God still was preparing me. The message was clear. No matter how hard you try, you can't outrun your purpose or destiny. It will still find you.

7

---

## Growing Pains

TEMPORARY DISCOMFORT EQUATES TO GROWTH, right? Starting a lymphedema program meant lots of changes for me. I am a libra with a type-A personality. I strive for balance in all things. I thrive when things are routine and I get stressed when things are out of order. I cannot function in chaos and dysfunction. I am a bit of a perfectionist. I was a newly trained lymphedema therapist and I felt very green. I was not at all confident in my treatments and patient care in this area. Everything was new—a new certification, a new program, and novice experience. All eyes were on me.

I had a very challenging experience with my department supervisor at the time. She was not knowledgeable about the inner workings of the lymphedema program and the supplies and documentation needed to start the program. We bumped heads constantly. One day, we were standing by the printer in the department discussing some aspects of the lymphedema program. She kept undermining my suggestions about the program.

I had enough. I finally said to her, "Do you not trust my judgment about this?"

She stared blankly at me for a minute then said, "Okay, I need to back off a little. I trust you know what you are doing."

The program and processes were still being developed, but my supervisor wanted to hire a new occupational therapist. To my surprise, this therapist was already a certified lymphedema therapist. I initially viewed this as a threat. The timing of it all was suspicious to me. I shifted my mind to try to see it as God's blessing in disguise. Besides, she already had two years of lymphedema experience and could be very helpful. This occupational therapist was not actively seeking a new job, but a cancer patient she was treating was very impressed with the care she received at my healthcare organization and told the OT that she would be a greater asset for my organization. It worked out that my supervisor got the position created so that the OT could join our staff. The OT came in for an interview which I sat in on. I specifically mentioned to her that our lymphedema program was under development and that it would possibly be a few months before we had our first patient. The OT said that she was okay with this. Ultimately, the OT was hired, but she quickly became unhappy working in acute care and not treating lymphedema patients. My supervisor not only suggested but insisted that we treat lymphedema patients on an inpatient basis, which I knew would not work for several reasons. First of all, lymphedema patients need consistent follow-up. Most average lengths of stay in the hospital are two to three days, which is not sufficient time to establish a treatment regime with adequate follow-up. Second of all, acute care patients are usually medically fragile. Certain medical conditions are contraindicated for lymphedema treatment, such as active infection, acute congestive heart failure exacerbation, and kidney failure/severe kidney dysfunction. Nonetheless, the OT was allowed to treat patients on an inpatient basis. I had to scramble to undo the situation and notify the attending hospital physicians and wound care nurse that it was best for patients to receive outpatient lymphedema treatment once they were more medically stable and able to be seen on a consistent basis.

As we began to market the program, we got a call for our first lymphedema patient to treat in the outpatient clinic. The documentation still had not adequately been established, however, we had just gotten the necessary treatment supplies in place. My supervisor basically left me without a say in the matter and let the OT treat the patient. There was another problem with this situation. Because we were two different disciplines, physical therapy and occupational therapy, we could not share the same patients. If something happened and either of us had to miss work for the day, the patients would be unable to be seen. For example, being that we were two different disciplines, if the OT missed work, in order for me—as a PT—to treat her patient, I would have to do a whole new PT evaluation on the patient in order to properly bill and charge for the services rendered. At the facility where this OT previously worked, her colleague was also an OT, which did not pose this problem for her.

Four months later, the OT decided to leave our hospital due to "personal reasons." In my opinion, I felt that she left because she was not treating lymphedema patients as much as she thought she would be. The supervisor's plan had backfired. The manner in which the OT was hired was not done in a way that was pleasing and again, I felt that she was trying to snub me. The reason? I did not know. This OT was promised that she would have a full patient load quickly and it turns out that she did not.

*Well, there goes my backup!* was the initial thought I had. Then I took a minute and thought, *Okay, God, sometimes you move people out of the way so that others can see that it's your Glory, and not other people.*

# Phase Two
## Life Lessons in Trauma, Tragedy, Faith, Spirituality, and Love

## 8

## Early Trauma

I LEARNED ABOUT FAMILY TRAUMA AT AN EARLY AGE. My mom was raised in a traumatic environment. My grandmother raised four boys and four girls and a granddaughter and endured a toxic marriage to my grandfather, who was an alcoholic. My mom would tell me stories about how Grandpa was a hard worker during the week and as cool as a cucumber during the weekdays. Her and her sisters learned how to cook by having to fix his lunch and dinner every day. On Friday evenings, my mom mentioned how anxiety would overtake them all because they knew when Grandpa got home on Fridays, he would get drunk and raise hell. He and Grandma would fuss and fight all night. My aunts and uncles frequently fled the house because of the disturbance. To this day, I feel that each one of them dealt with childhood trauma differently through means such as alcoholism, drug use, incarceration, children by multiple women in non-committed relationships, gambling, people-pleasing, or by being overly spiritual or overly controlling. Usually, at family gatherings, it was like my mom, aunts, and uncles spoke in code. They'd say, "I remember how it was back then," then someone else would say, "Yeah, I remember." One of my uncles would say, "Y'all left me, knowing how it was back then." My sisters and cousins and I often looked at each other with confused expressions, trying to figure out what they were talking about, but no one would ever say. All I know is, generational hurt, trauma, and pain are real.

My first experience with trauma was when my great aunt passed away. I was six years old. She became very ill and was diagnosed with a form of bone cancer. Even though I was young, it hurt me to see my aunt in so much pain and having to rely on others to help her. She would lie in bed mostly and sleep. She had gotten to the point of not being able to bathe herself. My middle sister and I would go to her house and I would watch my sister bathe her, lotion her up, and put powder wherever she wanted. Auntie loved body powder!

I didn't know what it was at the time, but I remember her having a bag attached to her. I now know that it was a urinary catheter. When I heard that she had passed away, I felt like everything was a blur. I remember the family gathering at my parents' house. I specifically remember one of my aunts sitting next to the piano in the living room crying.

The day of her funeral was weird. It was gray, dismal, and cloudy outside. She passed away not long before her birthday, which was on May 1. I don't think I quite understood what death was all about before then. I remember sitting on the front pew at her funeral, staring at the casket with her still body. Tears rolled down my face. I don't remember who tried to console me, I just remember thinking, "What am I going to do without my great auntie?" She was gone, and never coming back. The woman who I always thought was the strongest woman ever was not strong enough to win her battle against cancer. Playing in her front yard and scouring the ground for acorns from the huge oak tree that towered over the house would never be the same. Who would rub my back with green rubbing alcohol when my back itched? Who would tell me to come back inside of the house and get a snack after an hour of lying in the grass and looking up at the clouds in the sky? Who would stock the deep freezer with my favorite popsicles and ice cream? I would no longer be able to smell the aroma of dinner being prepared coming from the front door when getting off of the school bus. I would no longer be able to hear her voice calling me her "fat gal" as she gently patted my thigh. It wasn't until I was older that I realized the significant role she played in my life. Auntie loved me wholeheartedly and treated me as if I was her child. Outside of my parents and sisters, she was my first experience with unconditional love.

I experienced trauma again as I was a little older when my oldest sister and I experienced a blatant act of racism. It was unforgettable. We'd gone to a local dollar store in town where we normally went shopping. We were looking for comforter sets and bedroom decor. As my sister was in one aisle, I went to another aisle where the shoes were located. I didn't see anything of interest, so I went back to where my sister was. She picked up a few items and we checked out. We put the bags in the car and left and went to another dollar store in town. As we were getting out of the car, a police officer jumped out and stated that he needed to search the car.

"Why?" my sister asked. "We haven't done anything wrong."

The officer said we fit the description of someone who had stolen items from the dollar store that we had just left. We were both confused and obliged the officer and let him freely search the car because we knew it had to be a mistake. We asked what was reportedly taken and he said, "Ked-like canvas tennis shoes." We also both showed him our IDs. I was a junior in high school at the time. Of course, the officers did not find any shoes in the car, only the items that were paid for. He let us be on our way after that.

My sister was in a rage. The next day, she went back to the store to confront the manager of the store who made the accusation. One of my classmates worked at the store and said to the manager, "Crystal would never steal anything. She will be the valedictorian of our class." It made my sister even angrier and she let the store manager have it. The manager tried to apologize, but it was not enough for my sister. She even wrote an editorial in the local newspaper about the horrible experience. When all was said and done, it was discovered that the store manager's sister was the one who took the shoes and blamed it on me. Racial profiling at its finest, is it not? What goes around comes around. Not long after that incident, the dollar store closed down. Go figure. As the older generation used to say, "God don't like ugly."

Trauma struck once again. My oldest sister tried to commit suicide not once, but *twice*. The first time, I remember she was about to graduate from high school and found out that her boyfriend was cheating on her. She was so in love with him. Shortly after graduation, she attempted to cut her wrists. She had a history of being in toxic relationships. I never really liked any of the guys she brought around the family.

The racial profiling incident at the dollar store was one more thing that pushed her over the edge, causing her to sink into a dark place. It was New Year's Eve, 1999. My entire family was at home. We made party food and punch to celebrate bringing in the new year. We had a nice time. Shortly after the clock struck twelve, we all went to bed. I shared a bedroom with my middle sister. Early the next morning on New Year's Day, I heard a loud thud. It woke me and my sister up. We both jumped out of bed and went to my parents' room, which was right across the hall. They were both still sleeping. My oldest sister had her own room. We opened the door, and, to our dismay, saw her lying on the floor, barely responsive. I remember trying to wake her up and I kept calling her name saying, "Please get up." We saw an empty bottle of champagne and a bottle of pills next to the headboard of the bed. My middle sister went to wake up my mom and dad. They came into the room, and I went to the phone and called 911 for help. The local EMS responder came to our house. Slowly, my sister started to awaken, but was very groggy and slurring her words. I will never forget the image of the first responders putting her on the stretcher and wheeling her out of the front door to go to the local hospital. We all got dressed and went to the hospital. To our surprise, when we got to the hospital, a few family members were already there. Turns out they heard over a radio scanner that EMS had been sent to our residence, so they assumed something was wrong and came to the hospital to find out because no one answered their phone calls. It was very embarrassing to my parents. My parents prided themselves on raising upstanding young women and could not face the fact that their oldest daughter was in so much pain that she wanted to escape this earth.

After a few hours at the local hospital, my sister was taken to Augusta, Georgia, to an inpatient psychiatric hospital. She was on suicide watch. She was only there for a few days, then called to say she wanted to come home. Even though Augusta was only an hour away from home, it seemed like the longest car ride ever to pick her up and take her home. I could never fathom in my mind why my sister wanted to take her life *twice*. We had a good childhood. She was well educated and was working on a master's degree at the time. It didn't make sense to me. I could only attribute it to the men in her life bringing her to an all-time low. To this day, I caution myself with relationships and refuse to let any man devalue me as a woman and make me feel or think that I am not enough.

Another traumatic incident for me was when a tornado ripped through White Plains on November 22, 1992. It is a day I will never forget. My oldest sister was away at Paine College, and my mom was at work because her job required her to work some weekends. Me, my dad, and middle sister had just gotten home from church. I remember in Sunday school that day my teacher told us to pray for all of the people in Alabama who were affected by tornadoes that passed through the area. I remember saying aloud, "I hope it doesn't come this way." Church service was done at one p.m. The air outside was very strange. The sky was an ugly gray, and the winds were picking up. My dad and I stopped at someone's house close to the church to drop something off, then headed home. My middle sister beat us home and decided she was going to wash her hair. I turned on the TV and started watching *Mouse on the Mayflower*. After all, Thanksgiving was right around the corner. I remember seeing tornado warnings for Greene County scrolling across the screen, but I was twelve at the time and not sure about the difference between a tornado watch and a warning.

My sister was curling her hair, then told my dad, "It sounds like an airplane keeps circling around the house." My dad went outside. He left the back door open. I remember him standing at the back door with both hands outstretched towards the sky and he was praying. He came back inside and said, "There is a tornado in the air out there. Turn everything off." We turned off all lights and electronics that were going at the time and went to the hallway, which was the most interior room of the house. After twenty minutes, we heard a little wind but nothing that seemed to make us worry. We left the hallway and looked out of the large kitchen window which had the best view to the backyard and the cow pasture in the back. Suddenly, all of the trees in the pasture leaned in the same direction, and a huge rush of wind came over the house. Not thinking, we ran down into the den instead of going back to the hallway and huddled under the antique piano against the wall. In retrospect that was not a safe place at all. I had my white stuffed rabbit that I won at an Easter egg hunt against my chest, hugging it tightly. After a few minutes, the winds subsided and everything was quiet. We could tell that we had lost power. We emerged from the den, back to the kitchen to look outside. There were a few limbs in the yard and the sky was still eerie and gray. There was no damage that we could see to our home or neighbor's homes. We were worried because we knew my mom was supposed to be home from work soon. It was close to three or four in the afternoon. She usually only kept her car phone on in case of emergency. About fifteen minutes later, after all was said and done, my mom pulled up in the driveway and entered the house.

She said, "I stopped at the video store in Siloam to rent some movies and a saw a bunch of ambulances and fire trucks headed this way. What happened?"

We told her a tornado had just passed through.

She said, "If I hadn't stopped at the store I probably would have driven right into it."

Shortly after, our house phone began ringing with phone calls from family and church members saying that the church had been damaged badly as well as the rest of White Plains. A man not even one-half mile down the road from our house was pinned under his house. The only thing left standing were the bushes in his front yard. We were in disbelief. We got reports that several houses around the church were damaged and one person was killed when her trailer wrapped around a tree. We were told that the road leading to the church was impassable and we would not be able to drive there to see the damage, so we had to wait until daylight the next day. We called my oldest sister and told her what happened and she immediately started crying and wanted to come home.

The next day we were still without power. School was canceled. My family and I went riding around to see the damage. We were in shock. There was debris everywhere. Our poor little town was badly damaged, everything from the gas station to the fire station to the post office. We already didn't have much of anything but it was all damaged. There was a First Baptist Church around the corner from my church. Their steeple had been blown off. The damage to my church and surrounding homes was unreal. When we arrived at the church, news helicopters were flying around. Church members had gathered outside of the church and some were crying. It was gut-wrenching to see. The church center where we had Vacation Bible School and church dinners was completely gone, minus the two trees that stood in front. One of the church's main walls with beautiful blue stained-glass windows with a yellow cross was completely collapsed. This was the same side of the church that my dad sat on in the deacons' corner. You could still see the pews with the collection plates underneath. Pretty much the entire roof of the sanctuary was blown off and all of the pews were knocked backward like dominoes. The front vestibule of the church was still standing, but you could not enter the sanctuary due to the debris blocking the door. The back choir rooms and choir stands were still standing, but the roof was heavily damaged and you could see insulation everywhere. We were so fortunate that we did not have an evening service or program that day, or there probably would have been substantial injuries or loss of life.

The church was established in 1867. That was a lot of history wiped away in a matter of minutes. Nobody knew about the little town of White Plains, but the EF-4 tornado (sustained winds of 166–200 mph) that ripped through the town that day put us on the map. We were on all major news outlets in the Metro Atlanta, Macon, and Augusta areas.

We had to rebuild our church from the ground up. In the interim, other local community churches allowed us to use their church building on Sundays that they did not have service until our church was rebuilt. We were able to preserve the other stained glass windows that were not damaged in the storm and we were able to find the original manufacturer. About a year later, the church was rebuilt and Second Baptist Church was stronger than ever!

To this day, whenever I see a tornado warning or watch for my area, I am always quite nervous and terrified and constantly watching the weather when watches or warnings occur.

# 9

## Tragedy Versus Faith (Round One)

THE YEAR 2014 IS WHAT I WOULD CONSIDER ONE OF the worst years of my life. It seemed as if one bad thing after another happened to my family and me. At the time, I didn't know how my family and I would make it through. In retrospect, even though it was hard, God was in the midst of it all and was preparing me and my family for something that we could not yet see. My faith was being tested and developed.

It all started in January 2014. I brought in the new year with bronchitis and borderline pneumonia. I had never been this sick. I was literally on the couch for four days and physically did not have the energy to do much of anything. My oldest sister was also ill at the same time with almost the same condition. It hurt just to talk or breathe. Once I got over my illness, I thought, "Okay, Crystal, your year cannot start off like this." About a week later, the Atlanta area was experiencing some of the coldest winter temperatures in a long time. It was such a hard freeze that a pipe in my house burst while I was at work. I had no idea what was happening. I was in a grocery store just up the street from my house when I kept receiving calls from an unknown caller on my phone, which subsequently turned out to be the Gwinnett County police department. I was asked to confirm my address and then the voice said, "Ma'am, you need to get home right away. There is water running out of the front of your house." Panic set in. I left my shopping cart in the store, full of groceries, and sped home. I felt like my car was up on two wheels because I was driving so fast! At home, the police and two of my neighbors were standing in front of my house. They were unable to locate the water shutoff outside my home. In horror, I saw water coming through my front door and running down my driveway. I opened the door to find water coming out of the ceiling in my foyer. The hardwood floor and carpet and entrance to my stairwell were soaked. I frantically found the water shutoff in my garage and turned off the water supply to my house. From the looks of things, I just knew the entire upstairs to my house was flooded. I ran upstairs to find that everything was dry. I had a burst pipe that supplied my spigot on the front of my house, which leaked into the foyer. What was I going to do? I was a single woman and nothing like this had ever happened to me before. After all of the stress of having my foyer and kitchen stripped down to the studs with continued freezing temperatures outside, loud fans in my home for two weeks to dry everything out, trying to search for a reliable contractor to repair my home, allowing them access to my home without being there because of work, and dealing with the insurance company, my home was finally restored and I could be comfortable again. While my home was being repaired, a snow/ice storm hit the area. This halted repair efforts on my home. To make matters worse, I had to sleep at the hospital for three days because I was stuck at work, scheduled to work, and, per hospital policy, I was not allowed to leave. Thank God the contractor and his team that I hired, knowing I was stuck at work, were honest men and even offered to take care of my home for me and continue to work.

After January, things continued to spiral downhill. In February, one of my dad's brothers passed away. He lost his battle with cancer and was previously on hospice care. In March, what I would consider the unthinkable happened. My grandmother had a stroke and was hospitalized. My family and I were devastated because my grandma was such a strong woman and had never been hospitalized other than having her knee replacement surgery.

Let me tell you a little more about my grandmother. She was a tough old bird. We did not know she had fallen at home and had a stroke. A neighbor called her to check in every day, but couldn't get my grandmother on the phone that particular day, so she decided to walk to my grandmother's house to see if she was okay. To her surprise, she knocked on the door and my grandmother crawled on the floor to get to the door to open it. The neighbor called my mom and told her what happened, and my grandmother was taken to the hospital. We kept trying to ask my grandmother what happened, but all she kept saying is that she tripped over a white box on the floor in her room. To our recollection, there was no white box on the floor.

I spent the first night in the hospital with my grandmother, trying to ensure she was comforted and also overseeing her care. She was confused and wanted to go home. She kept trying to get out of bed, setting the alarms off. I kept telling her everything would be okay. Once she knew that I was there with her and not leaving, she calmed down and drifted off to sleep. The next morning, the neurologist came in. He knew I was in the medical field, so he showed me my grandmother's MRI and CAT scan. She had a huge five-centimeter-by-three-centimeter bleed in the left parietal lobe in her brain with a significant midline shift, yet she was alive and able to walk in the halls on her rolling walker with the therapists. They diagnosed my grandmother with thin blood vessels in her brain and stated that the chances of her having another stroke were imminent, even after being prescribed medications to help. We discussed sending her to a rehab facility or hospice. My grandmother lived alone, and we knew that she would require close supervision and a lot of care after being discharged from the hospital. We all knew my grandmother loved being at home, so as a family, with my mom being her primary caregiver, she decided to keep my grandmother comfortable at home. She received in-home physical therapy and occupational therapy, nursing care, and we made sure she had all the equipment she needed to help with her mobility. My cousin, who my grandmother raised, even moved in to help out. After a while, my grandmother refused to eat and work with the therapists to improve her strength and endurance. It became increasingly difficult for my mom and cousin to take care of her. She gradually continued to decline physically.

April and May were relatively quiet compared to previous months, however, we found out that one of my mom's first cousins was diagnosed with two types of cancer, lung and prostate. His daughter was in Virginia and was not able to come to Georgia to help, so my mom stepped up to the plate. She took him to numerous doctor's appointments and chemotherapy appointments. In June, he passed away.

In July, my mom's oldest brother was hit by a car. No one knows for sure what happened, but it appeared to be a hit and run. He was taken to the hospital with multiple injuries and endured multiple surgeries. Eventually, he was placed in a nursing home and remained on a ventilator, leaving him with a poor quality of life and significant impairment to his mobility. I went to visit him. I almost wish I hadn't, seeing him lying there in that condition. He was pretty much unresponsive, not even able to make his needs known. That's not how I wanted to remember him.

In September, my grandmother suffered what we think was another stroke and went back to the hospital. We discussed hospice again and, even though my mother did not want to put my mother into hospice or in a nursing home, this was the best decision. My grandmother always said she never wanted to be put in a nursing home. This hurt my mother to the core and to this day, it still does, but she had to place my grandmother in the hands of qualified healthcare workers for her to get the care she needed. My grandmother stayed in the nursing home for two weeks, then passed away September 15, 2014, at the age of ninety-one. I was on my way to work that morning when around seven thirty a.m., my mom called and said, "Momma passed around five a.m. this morning." I pulled over into the Publix parking lot up the street from my house and broke down in tears. I was so heartbroken. I always viewed my grandmother as invincible and I just knew that she would live to be over one hundred years old. She endured an abusive marriage, raised eleven children, eight of her own and three grandchildren, two of which she began raising while she was in her seventies. Her funeral was September 21, 2014, just two days before my thirty-third birthday. How could my grandmother be gone? She was my inspiration and my whole reason for becoming a physical therapist. She supported me throughout college and would always give me money when I came home to visit her, slipping twenty-dollar bills into my hand when nobody else could see. I would no longer be able to hear her voice saying, "Hey, baby, I'm doing all right." I would no longer see the smile on her face from the joy she felt when her family gathered for the holidays, especially Mother's Day and Christmas.

We had to help with her funeral arrangements. My sisters and I chose pictures and wrote her obituary while my mom handled the other aspects of the funeral arrangements, including deciding how to dress my grandmother, the casket color, and how my grandmother's hair would be styled. I dreaded going to her wake. She looked beautiful, but it still did not take away the pain that I felt. My mom was incredibly strong. She barely even shed a tear. I was not looking forward to her funeral. It did not seem real. My oldest sister wrote a beautiful tribute to my grandmother and read it at the funeral. After the funeral, I went back to my grandmother's house to get my car. We were all going to gather at my mom's house afterward. As I walked back to my car, a pretty yellow and black butterfly followed me and landed right on the car door in front of me. I immediately felt my grandmother's presence and that she was okay and everything was going to be okay. Even now, whenever I think of her, I typically see yellow butterflies. It's her way of letting me know she is still around.

A few days after the funeral, I had a dream about my grandmother. We were at the funeral again. However, she was sitting in the pulpit with the preacher overseeing everything. She was nodding her head in approval of her service.

I still feel the heartbreak as if it just happened yesterday.

A week later, after my grandmother's funeral, I was supposed to go to Charlotte to be in my friend's wedding. We graduated from physical therapy school together and had become quite close. It was so hard for me to attend the rehearsal dinner and wedding ceremony and be happy for her when I had just lost my grandmother. "This too shall pass" is what I had to keep telling myself, even though I drove to Charlotte and back home in tears.

A few weeks later, my dad's sister passed away. She was in her seventies and, a few years before, was treated for breast cancer. Her daughter said that my aunt was sick and had a cough that would not go away and she did not want to go back to a hospital. My aunt was taken to the hospital, then passed away the same day from what we think was a recurrence of her breast cancer. In a two-week time frame, I lost my grandmother, celebrated my thirty-third birthday (in which I did not do anything other than stay home because I was still grieving my grandmother), witnessed the wedding of a friend, then lost an aunt. By that point, I was emotionally spent.

In October, one of my uncles was having chest pain. He was taken to the hospital, then sent home. He began having chest pains again and went back to the hospital. This time, he needed open heart surgery and ended up having a triple bypass.

In December, my uncle who had been hit by a car in July passed away. The funeral was held on Christmas Eve, which was also my aunt's and his sister's birthday. Just the thought of having to endure another funeral around the holidays made my stomach turn. Why do I write this? My mom had lost two brothers around Christmas time. In December 2006, I graduated from physical therapy school. I was living with my oldest sister at the time in Augusta and was in the process of studying to take my licensure exam as well as was going on various job interviews in the Atlanta area. On Christmas Eve, around three a.m., my sister woke me up.

"Two of our uncles got killed in a car accident," she said.

What did she just say to me? I was in a fog and it took me a few minutes to process what she was saying. She said it again.

"Both of them?" I said. "At the same time?" I was at a loss for words. These were my mom's brothers. Even today we don't know all the details, but they were a few miles from home. They were coming around a curve and swerved to avoid another car. One uncle was ejected from the vehicle and killed at the scene. The other died by the time he reached the hospital. We immediately called my parents and my first cousins. My grandmother was in Atlanta visiting for the Christmas holiday at my aunt's house and had gotten the news. My aunt and my grandmother had to go to the hospital to identify the bodies. My sister and I drove home to my parents' house the next morning. As we were leaving her apartment, we noticed a flock of black buzzards around her car and in the parking lot. It felt like death as we walked outside. My sisters and I had to help my mom write her brother's obituaries, pick out caskets, and flowers. December 31, New Year's Eve, my family and I attended a double funeral.

My uncle's sons said that they were supposed to go with my uncles that night, but decided not to. So glad they didn't. We may have been looking at four caskets instead of two. So this is why I wrote earlier that having to endure another funeral around the Christmas holidays was terrible.

The year of 2014 was indeed horrible. I was so broken but I put on the facade that I was okay. Everybody in my family looked to me to be the strong one. Little did they know I was in pieces. "Strong As Glass", a song by neo-soul artist Goapele, resonated in my head as I thought back over 2014, the worst year of my life as well as other failures and experiences I have aforementioned. I began to think, 2014 was a year of loss, but yet symbolic of when something is lost, something better is to be gained.

*10*

## Tragedy Versus Faith (Round Two)

THE YEARS OF 2015 AND 2016 WERE BETTER. I HAD obtained my lymphedema certification in 2016 and the program at my hospital was up and running. Things were good, and I thanked God for it. The holidays came and there were no major family issues. Thanksgiving was good. I spent it with my immediate family, and we had a wonderful time. All was well.

On December 5, one of my sister's called me and said, "I think Mom was in a bad accident." She said she was scrolling on her Facebook page and saw a post from the Greene County fire department. It looked like her car, but I refused to believe it. I said, "No, that can't be her car." If it was, by the looks of it, whoever was in both cars surely did not make it out of that accident alive. Both cars were a mangled mess. We both tried to call my parents' house several times but there was no answer. My brother-in-law called both the police department and the fire department, but they wouldn't give him information. My sister tried to call my cousin, who lived around the corner from my parents, to go and see if their car was at home.

She was unable to get a hold of her. Finally, my brother-in-law was able to get some answers from the fire department and was told that it was my mother who was in the accident and that she had been taken to the hospital. Sheer panic set in. We did not know what happened, what condition she was in, how my dad was handling everything, or how the other driver was doing. Even though I felt numb, I was able to think clearly enough to call the hospital. They would not give me any other information other than that my mother was at the emergency room. I was able to get my dad on the phone at the hospital. He said she had a broken wrist and two broken ribs. Turns out that she blacked out behind the wheel while coming home from the pharmacy. She said she did not feel well, and all of a sudden, she was unable to see how to get over or turn on her blinkers. She said all she remembered was pressing the button to activate the emergency system in her car, then woke up to two men telling her to get out of the car. She was able to walk out of the car. Lord have mercy! My mom had a hypoglycemic episode, and it was also determined that she had a urinary tract infection or UTI. Working at a hospital, I knew all too well that a UTI can cause disorientation and confusion. My mom had passed out before when she had a bad UTI. She was treated and released from the hospital the same night. All I remember is trying to get home as fast as possible. It was dark and it was raining heavily the whole hour-and-a-half drive home, and my oldest sister and my brother-in-law were on their way to my parents' house from Augusta. My sisters and I were on a three-way call, trying to keep each other calm.

When I got to my parents' house, I rushed inside. They were sitting at the kitchen table. My mom, trying to eat, had one arm in a sling. Dad was sitting next to her. She looked as if nothing ever happened. I burst into tears. To hear my dad recall how he got the news that she had been in an accident was absolutely heartbreaking. My focus was making sure my mom was comfortable and okay. Apparently, X-rays determined that she sustained a fracture of her right wrist and had two broken ribs on her right side. My mom was right-handed, so she now had to rely on her left hand to do everything.

I took a few days off work and took my mom to an appointment with an orthopedic doctor. They took X-rays again and put her arm in a cast. The doctor said that she should stay in the cast for at least six weeks and then he would reevaluate. Unfortunately, nothing could be done for the broken ribs other than pain meds and proper positioning. The physical therapist in me kicked in. I made sure my mom was positioned correctly when she was sitting and trying to lie down in bed. My dad and brother-in-law retrieved a lift recliner from my grandmother's house and put it in the family room for my mom to easily get up and down. I printed out exercises for her shoulder, elbow, and hand to keep swelling down and to prevent loss of her range of motion. I made sure she was using her incentive spirometer to take deep breaths so that she would not develop pneumonia. It was painful for her to take a deep breath, but it was necessary to keep her lungs open and clear. I also taught her how to use a pillow on her side if she had to cough and sneeze. I had to teach her a new way to put on her bra and how to wrap her casted arm in a garbage bag to prevent the cast from getting wet in the shower. My mom is very independent, so she quickly adapted and began doing everything with her left hand. My experience working in the hospital definitely helped me to help my mom through this difficult time.

My mom was worried sick about the other guy who was injured in the crash. Fortunately, the guy was someone another family member knew. He was in his twenties. We were given an update that he was hospitalized for a short time but then released home. The family did not pursue charges but simply allowed the insurance companies from both sides to handle the expenses incurred from the accident. My mom developed a great fear of driving. If my sisters and I were not present, my dad made sure to drive her wherever she needed to go. He would jokingly say, "I have been driving Miss Daisy!"

My oldest sister and I work really hard, so we usually take a sister's trip once a year. We decided to go to Cancún, Mexico, for a little R and R after Christmas. We both felt guilty for going, especially being that my mom was in a car accident and was not 100 percent healed, but she insisted we not cancel plans because of her. My dad was there with her, and my other sister was also on standby if they needed her. We went to Cancún, tried to enjoy ourselves, but we could not shake what had happened to my mom. We called home and checked on her every day. We tried to enjoy ourselves as much as we could, then returned home to my parents' house to spend New Year's with them. We brought in the New Year in prayer for a prosperous New Year and to thank God for His blessings and the blessings yet to come.

We were all awakened at five a.m. to the sound of the phone ringing, quickly followed by the sound of my mother crying. We got a phone call that my thirty-one-year-old cousin had a medical emergency and had died at the hospital. All we knew was that he stopped breathing and was unable to be revived. My maternal grandmother raised my cousin and his sister in her seventies. We grew up together. We thought we had escaped this holiday season unscathed by death, yet here was death knocking on my family's door again. I cannot get the sounds out of my head of my mother crying hysterically. My dad was teary-eyed trying to console her. My sister could only shake her head in disbelief, unable to show any emotion. I was crying. My brother-in-law also had a disbelieving, somber look. Even my sister's dog tried to console my mom.

After my grandmother died, she made my mom the executor of her estate. My grandmother held the life insurance policy for my cousin, and my mother was responsible after my grandmother's death. Because of this, my mom was responsible for making all of the funeral arrangements. My sisters and I helped to write the obituary and find the picture to put on the front. We also had the daunting task of once again, going to the funeral home to pick out a casket. Unbelievable! We had experienced so much death that we jokingly said we should open up our own funeral business because we had so much experience in planning funerals.

The funeral was the Saturday after New Year's. It was cold and rainy with snow mixed in. We made it through the funeral.

My cousin was going to be buried next to his dad (who was killed in 2006 on Christmas Eve in a car accident), my grandmother, and all the others we lost in 2014. I was still raw from my other family deaths. I broke down and cried uncontrollably, almost falling to the ground. My sisters and aunt tried to console me, but I could only say, "This is just too much." How could a thirty-one-year-old have his life ended this way?

It took us a while to obtain the autopsy results. During this process, I had a vivid dream about my grandmother. My mom and I were at my grandmother's house sitting on the bed in her room. She was sitting in the pink recliner in her room laughing and talking on the phone, almost in a flirtatious manner with a cardiologist. Upon waking up from the dream, I said to myself, "Why in the world did I dream of my grandmother talking to a cardiologist on the phone?" About three days later, my cousin's nephew, who was a police officer, called and said the autopsy results were in. My cousin had passed away from an enlarged heart. That's it! My grandmother was trying to tell me he had a heart condition in the dream, hence her being on the phone with a cardiologist. "Wow," was all I could say. Even though she was gone, she still tried to communicate with me to give us some sort of peace and closure about the situation.

*11*

---

## Seasonal Yet Purposeful People

WE HAVE ALL HEARD THE SAYING, "I WAS IN THE right place at the right time" or "some people come into your life for a season." This has certainly been true in my life. But through all of these encounters, a lesson was learned, and these experiences helped me become the woman I am today. I firmly believe nothing happens by chance and every person we encounter is put in our lives by God. There are no mistakes, only life lessons. Now I will share with you some experiences and lessons I have had in the area of love and relationships.

I graduated from undergrad in 2004 and moved to Augusta to live with my oldest sister because I was about to start physical therapy school in the fall and had a summer internship to complete there. During that summer, I met a guy who was in the army and was stationed in Killeen, Texas. At the time we met, he was in Augusta visiting his family while he was on vacation. We hit it off well. We spent a lot of time together in a short amount of time and I thought he was the perfect gentleman. We talked and hung out every day for two weeks straight. He had to leave to go back to Texas and I was so sad. I really liked him so we kept in touch and decided to see how a long-distance relationship would work. We talked every day and every night. Once I started PT school, he transferred to Ft. Eustis in Virginia Beach, Virginia. He drove down to see me whenever he got two-week breaks and on holidays. When I was on break from school, he flew me up to Virginia to see him. He was the sweetest guy. He supported me financially while I was in school. Being a broke college student was no fun. He made sure I had money in my account and bought me a new computer when my laptop gave up the ghost.

Once I graduated from PT school, my boyfriend made it clear that he was going to remain in the army but wanted to move to be closer to me and his family, so he reenlisted and was stationed in Ft. Benning in Columbus, Georgia. I attempted to find a job in Columbus and went on several interviews, but none worked out. Deep in my heart, I always wanted to live in Atlanta, so I pursued that. I would be almost two hours away from Columbus, but it was a heck of a lot closer than him being in Virginia. If we could make it work being over eight hours away, surely we could make it work being just two hours away.

We were together for a total of five years. In that time, he was deployed to Iraq two times. We wrote and emailed each other, and he called me whenever he could, sometimes in the wee hours of the morning. I heard loud noises in the background and asked him, "What was that?"

"Oh, nothing to worry about," he'd say.

I knew it was the sound of explosions, but he tried to keep me from worrying and panicking that he was not safe. After his second deployment, the dynamics between us began to change. Our relationship went south quickly. The stress of PT school and being worried about him being in Iraq took a toll on me and I began eating more and gained weight. One time when he came home, he said to me, "You need to lose some weight," and looked at me as if I disgusted him. In all the time we spent together, he never said anything like that to me before. It was like he changed. I found some evidence on three different occasions that he was cheating on me. One night we got into an argument. We were yelling and screaming so loud that the neighbors called the cops. He raised his hands near my throat as if he was about to hit me or choke me and I lost it! I was swinging and punching him relentlessly. I was determined to hurt him before he hurt me. The only thing he could do to stop me was lay me on the floor and pin me down to control me. That was the last straw for me. I felt that I was settling. I was done with the insecurity, cheating, and him breaking my confidence as a woman. It was time to move on. Lesson learned: don't settle for someone you are not happy with and never let anyone lessen your self-worth. If you don't know your value, no one else will!

IN 2015, I began to get a little depressed about being a single, professional, woman in the Atlanta dating scene. I was financially stable, outgoing, and educated with no kids. Why was dating so hard? I was a successful woman. However, success doesn't keep you warm at night or greet you when you wake up in the morning or come home from work in the evenings. Don't get me wrong. I went on lots of dates, but the guys were not who I was looking for. Or all they wanted was to wine and dine me a few times and then have sex. That was not at all what I wanted. Just as I was about to give up on dating, I met a guy. For our first date, we went to an Italian restaurant, something simple and convenient for both of us. He was such a gentleman. He showed up with a bouquet, opened doors for me, and paid for dinner. Not to mention he was tall, dark, very attractive, had no kids, and was well educated. He had a bachelor's degree in Mechanical Engineering and was currently in school to obtain an MBA. He was also a motivational speaker. The conversation was great, and he was an excellent communicator. He never left a text message unanswered, and I never had to wonder about the effort he was putting forth to get to know me and spend time with me. He would always leave me motivational cards in my car and bring me flowers weekly. He also gave me a book by Joel Osteen that we began to read together called *You Can, You Will*. As we read the book, we both made and updated our vision boards. We were both on the same page with wanting to fulfill our purpose to help others using our God-given talents. We prayed together before starting our workday and sent each other inspirational quotes during the day. We had a great bond that developed into a relationship.

I shared with him my goal of having my own successful jewelry business. He saw some of the handmade pieces I had, and immediately told me to go for it! Within two months, I had formed an LLC for my company and obtained a business license. He gave me great ideas regarding marketing and logos and helped me to design the logo for my jewelry company. We definitely inspired each other.

One day, there was a luncheon at his school, Kennesaw State University, and he invited me to come. A speaker was also present for one of their classes. She had launched her own lingerie company and was a self-made millionaire. He told me, "You have to meet her." He also told me to take off the handmade necklace that I was wearing (made by me), go to the dollar store and get a gift box, and give it to her. I complied because I trusted his judgment. The hustle was on!

Frantically, I ran to the local dollar store, found a gift box, took off my necklace, packaged it nicely, and made it back in time for the Q and A with the speaker. I went up to her, introduced myself, and placed the gift box in her hand. I could tell I made a memorable impression because I was the only person to give her something personal. After a brief conversation, she gave me her personal contact information. I reached out to her later and she led me to a contact who was president of the board of directors for Susan G. Komen Greater Atlanta. I reached out to this contact and ended up serving on the host committee for a fundraiser called Jeffrey Fashion Cares, which raised money for the Atlanta AIDS fund and Susan G. Komen. Upon talking with her, she was more interested in the fact that I was a physical therapist who was newly certified in lymphedema as she was a breast cancer survivor. This led to another contact, the chairman of the grants committee for Susan G.

Komen and the director of breast imaging for the healthcare organization I was currently working for. I began to think, "Okay, God, what are you really trying to tell me here?" I began thinking about all the people who had told me I should have my own practice. *God, are You trying to tell me it's not about me having my own jewelry business? Are You urging me to work with cancer patients in my area and not make jewelry my main focus?*

Shortly after, I connected with the lingerie businesswoman again inadvertently. I was on the website of a local business that focused on women-owned businesses, teaching how to obtain business funding. The company was hosting a session with an investment company that was owned by the lingerie businesswoman.

Upon arrival, I realized I was the only one there. I got a one-hour one-on-one session with her and her husband. She remembered me from our first encounter at KSU. I had more jewelry samples and pictures of my work to show her in addition to a website I had created. Needless to say, she was very impressed.

Her husband was there. He was a cancer survivor of stage three adenocarcinoma and had written a book about how he dealt with his cancer diagnosis, including receiving chemotherapy. I had a copy of the book and he signed it for me.

My boyfriend couldn't finish his degree at KSU for financial reasons, but he said, "If nothing else comes from that semester of me being at KSU, I hope that contact you met in my class leads you somewhere."

I was in the process of becoming lymphedema certified. Because of the intensity of this certification, I decided to put the jewelry business on hold. My spirit was telling me to focus my efforts on lymphedema and cancer care. My boyfriend even made a drawing on a yellow piece of notebook paper and wrote that I would have my own lymphedema treatment center. I took the piece of paper, folded it up, and placed it in my Bible. It was something I was praying on.

Our connection was intense. We had similar goals, drive, and ambition. We were like twin souls. The mental stimulation was impeccable. We would often see each other's birthdays, especially when looking at the clock. He would often see 9:23 (my birthday is September 23) and I would often see his birthday, 8:22 (August 22). It happened frequently. What did it all mean? What was this connection? I researched what the number sequences meant and came to the conclusion that all of the synchronicities I was experiencing were revealing to me that it was *my time* to do what God set out for me to do.

Our relationship progressed very fast. We were spending a lot of time together, which was really different for me because I was so accustomed to being by myself and spending time alone. It was almost to the point of being overwhelming. We were both independent and strong-minded individuals and after about three months, our personalities began to clash big time. I was an alpha female, and he was an alpha male. It caused communication breakdown. I felt like I could no longer say the right thing or express what I was feeling without him being offended or taking it the wrong way. Long story short, our goals and dreams outweighed the idea of actually being in a relationship and getting to really know each other. The idea and concept of a relationship seemed nice and the proverbial list of qualities in a potential mate may have looked good on paper. At the end of the day, though, I learned that not everyone that crosses your path is meant for you to be in a relationship with and you have to learn when a person has served their purpose in your life. What can you take away from that person crossing your path? It may be for that person to help you realize your purpose and to help propel you to the next level.

We ended our relationship and not exactly on the best of terms. I was brutally honest with him and expressed some things I was not happy with. I could tell I broke his ego. I knew I had. I felt that he had this idealistic vision of a relationship and who he thought I should be and was constantly comparing me to other women he has previously been in relationships with.

He wanted to remain friends, and we tried to be friends, but I felt that it was difficult to maintain that boundary between friends and being in a relationship as I felt that he still placed expectations on me as if we were still in a relationship.

Later, I thought, "We had so much passion and fire for each other before, maybe it's worth a second shot." He occasionally texted me, but I did not respond to the texts because I was reluctant to return to the past. Besides, I already felt like a failure with that relationship and did not want to deal with it again. However, a small voice kept saying, "Maybe you should just try again and see where it leads."

In that time apart, several things he and I talked about in our relationship were constantly being revealed to me. I thought back to how we would often watch Joel Osteen together. There were lots of moments of us gasping and looking at each other with eyes wide open, as Joel confirmed through his messages, conversations that we just had about life and what we thought was our calling and God-given purpose. One day we were watching an episode of *Super Soul Sunday*. That day, Oprah was interviewing Charles Shultz, the CEO of Starbucks. One thing he said really spoke to me. He said, "Do what you do with a purpose." He shared his inspiring story of how he was turned down two hundred times to receive financing to grow his business, and how eventually he raised the money to purchase Starbucks for over $3 million as he did not have the funds to do so. He was persistent.

April 16, 2016, I began reading a book written by my cousin titled *While I Wait: An Inspirational Guide for Single and Divorced Women in Their Season of Waiting*. I thought about the significance of the timing of her book release. It came at a time just as I was beginning to figure out what my purpose was. She posed several thought-provoking points:

> "If you are single and engaged to be married, I strongly encourage you to diligently seek God about your mate. If you do not know your purpose, seek God for clarity about it and make sure that the man you are in a relationship with has purpose in your life and is connected to your God-given purpose."[1]

---

[1] Candace B. Woods, *While I Wait: An Inspirational Guide for Single and Divorced Women in Their Season of Waiting*, 2016.

Hmmm... I was reading this at a time when I was considering reentering a relationship with someone who was connected to my purpose. I finally responded to him, and we met up. We talked and got reacquainted over a game of air hockey. We started hanging out more and he told me that he still loved me and had feelings for me. I could not reciprocate those exact words, but I did say, "Let's just see where this goes."

After a few months of trying to rekindle what we thought was left of our connection, I decided that our relationship had run its course. He told me that he was caught between me and another woman, but both of us women had qualities that he wanted. I was not going to play second fiddle to anyone. He gave me this story about how he had history with the other woman, they had been friends for a very long time, she was very supportive, took care of more things at home but was not ambitious enough, blah blah blah. On the other hand, he had more chemistry with me and loved my ambition and I motivated him to want to become better, blah blah blah. I gave him the deuces at that point. Either you want Crystal for Crystal or not, no in-between. I know my self-worth and will not place the destiny of my love life into the hands of someone who gives that facade that he has his business together and knows what he wants but ultimately is as confused as a bed bug. Here I was once again with him, being compared to someone else. I was done and over it. Boy, bye! On to the next!

Unfortunately, that meant that his purpose in my life had already been served. I tend to shy away from things that I feel are hurtful to me or things that I have failed at. Here I went again, another failed relationship. Even though we had this intense connection, ultimately the whole relationship was about a lesson in purpose. We were not meant to be in a relationship. We were meant to inspire each other to reach new heights and find our purpose. It was time to move on. His purpose had been served.

IN 2012, I underwent a weight loss transformation. I had lost fifty pounds and was feeling great! I wanted to take my fitness up a notch and joined a local gym. I signed up with a personal trainer. He was very cool and laid back, not to mention very easy on the eyes. He was older, no kids, and had never been married. We often talked during our training sessions about life and horrible dating experiences, but that relationship never developed beyond just speaking to each other at the gym in a trainer/client relationship. After several years in 2015, he began to show interest. He remembered my birthday and many other intimate details we discussed with each other from years before. He noticed that I always kept to myself. I chose to just be friends with him.

In 2016, I was diagnosed with a uterine polyp. I had irregular menstrual bleeding which was very annoying. I felt as if I was having a menstrual cycle every two weeks. The polyp had to be surgically removed and my doctor told me that if it wasn't, it could cause me to miscarry if I ever tried to get pregnant. My mom and sisters were unable to assist me, and my other friends were all working. I needed someone to take me to my surgery and take me home afterward.

I was still friends with my trainer at the time and told him about what was going on. Without hesitation he volunteered to take me to my surgery appointment. He was a good friend. He picked me up on time, made sure I got to the surgery safely, waited for me in the waiting room until I was done, and made sure I made it safely home. Even though we hung out from time to time, we never pursued a romantic relationship. However, he was just what I needed at the time. He was a reminder to me that there are good guys in the world who truly do value friendship with no strings attached.

I WAS FOND of a family friend, a close friend of one of my first cousins. I often saw him around the holidays because he always came to my aunt's house. He was a very eccentric guy who marched to the beat of his own drum. He was ex-military, well cultured, traveled all over the world, had a nonprofit children's foundation, and had a PhD. He had even written several books. He was tall, dark, and handsome. I had a crush on him. I had even gone on a trip with him, my cousin, and another one of her friends to

Puerto Rico. We flirted with each other whenever we were together. He intrigued me. I considered him a free spirit. Probably too free. What do I mean by this? I discovered that he did not believe in God but said he believed in a "higher power." He did not believe in celebrating birthdays and holidays. Hmmm . . . that really did not sit well with me. I was always taught not to be unequally yoked. Whenever I was with my cousins and family, we somehow always started talking about relationships. He also talked about how many women he had been with or other sexual encounters. Hmmm . . . is he really ready for a woman such as myself, who is settled and not promiscuous? Finally one year, he asked me for my number and expressed interest in me. He occasionally called, wanting to come over, but never once said, "Hey, Crystal, let me take you out." The calls were sporadic. A call one month, then I would not hear from him until three months later. I don't even know why I entertained him or the thought of possibly trying to develop something with him. He was very secretive. He even would rush me off the phone when my cousin was around as he did not want her to know that he and I were communicating. We played cat and mouse for a while. I love to travel, and he offered to be my travel buddy on my next trip. I considered it briefly, then my gut instinct kicked in and said, "Nah, I'm good!" I eventually got tired of the random phone calls that led nowhere. I did learn from him the steps needed to start my nonprofit organization, so that was a positive, but I still eventually cut him off. Lesson learned: don't try to force something to happen when your gut instinct is telling you "no," and never compromise your religious beliefs for anyone. It was time to move on. If somebody really values you and wants to be with you, you won't be a secret.

I RECONNECTED THROUGH social media with a guy I went to high school with. He kept sending messages to me showing interest. I kept dodging him but finally said, "Why not." I always thought he was cute in school when he would flirt with me. Nothing ever came of it because he had a girlfriend at the time. He also had an eight-year-old daughter. We met up at a lounge and had a conversation over a game of billiards. He shared with me how he had been through a lot of drama with his daughter's mom. Their communication with each other was horrible and had devolved into email communication only. He was cool, funny, and quick-witted. I was beginning to enjoy the time we spent together. We started hanging out more and more. One day I was chatting with him and his cousin about people we knew from our hometown. My brother-in-law was from the same town, so when I mentioned the name, he and his cousin's eyes got huge!

"Who did you say was your brother-in-law?" he said.

I said the name again.

"That is my dad's brother," he said.

Who would have known that after all of these years, I reconnect with him, and he would turn out to be my brother-in-law's nephew? What a small world! He did not have the greatest relationship with his dad, and my brother-in-law did not have the greatest relationship with his brother, so they had not seen each other in years. I couldn't wait to tell my sister the news! When I told her, she immediately told her husband, and we were all amazed. My brother-in-law said he had not seen his nephew and twin brother in ages. We tried dating, but after about a year I discovered he was not the one for me. Quite honestly, I was tired of hearing about that baby mama drama. He was a good dad and even helped take care of his niece and nephew, but we just were not meant to be long-term. The purpose for us crossing paths again was for me to reconnect him with family, not for him to be my life partner.

ON MARCH 16, 2018, I met a guy at a local restaurant that had live music every Friday night. I love live music, so I frequented the location often, especially because it was so close to my home. My girlfriend and I wanted some good food and cocktails and went to hear our favorite band performing that night. I was at a point in my life where I was completely over the dating scene. I had decided that I was going to just focus on myself and my career. We finally found a seat at the bar, ordered cocktails, and began looking over the menu.

An older dark-skinned gentleman came and sat at the bar next to my friend and overheard us trying to figure out what to order.

"Hmmm, what should we try?" I asked.

"The salmon is really good, and the lemon pepper wings," he said.

"Okay, thank you! Are you a regular here?" I asked.

"Something like that" he answered.

He continued to make small talk with my friend who eventually leaned over to me and said, "He is interested in you."

"Nah," I said. "He is totally not my type, plus I am not here to entertain any guys tonight. I am not in the mood."

Our food arrived and his food arrived. He was correct: the food was delicious. He even offered us to sample food from his plate. I declined but my girlfriend took him up on the offer.

Throughout the night she kept saying, "You need a man like that. He is very mature, calm, cool, collected, generous, has his own business, and he is interested. Forget that you don't think he is your type." She got up to go to the bathroom, so that left an empty seat between him and me. When my friend returned, she kept elbowing me to get up and move over a seat.

"Move over and talk to him!" she said.

"No!" I kept saying.

She finally gave me one last nudge and then I was like, "Okay." I moved over and we began to talk more, the typical questions you ask when you are meeting someone for the first time: "Where are you from? What do you like to do? Where do you normally like to hang out?" I always feel like it's a job interview (insert eye roll here).

He asked me what I did for a career, so I whipped out my business card and told him that I was a physical therapist specializing in lymphedema therapy and cancer rehab. He took the business card, pulled out a pen, and scratched out the logo of the company I worked for.

"Why don't you have your own business?" he said. "You are young. What are you waiting on?"

I felt an overwhelming peace in my spirit when he said it. I had recently been praying to God for Him to let me know if starting my own business should be my next move. And here I was at a lounge, sitting at a bar, talking to a stranger who offered me peace and confirmation. We talked, laughed, and danced the rest of the night and ultimately exchanged numbers. He was cool. He was not disrespectful in any way and was very encouraging. I went home that night, climbed into my bed, thinking about what had transpired. I thought to myself, "God, you send confirmation in the most unusual ways."

He stayed in my spirit for a few weeks. I decided to reach back out to him because I had not heard from him. He told me he was on a mission trip in Guatemala but wanted to see me as soon as he got back. We went back to the restaurant where we first met to hear more live music. We were inseparable after that. We began to spend more and more time together. He told me that on the night he first saw me, there was a "light" around me, which attracted him to me. We became friends, but the more time I spent with him, the more I liked him. He was a Christian man. I kept telling myself, "Nah, I can't possibly be falling for him." I used every excuse to deny the fact that I was falling in love with him: "He is older. He has three girls. I said I would never date anyone again with children. He is divorced. I said I would never date anyone divorced because they might have a lot of baggage. He isn't the typical guy I would go for in terms of appearance." Whenever I talked to him, I kept saying, "Hey, friend!" to minimize the fact that I was developing feelings for him. Our relationship progressed at a fast pace. I met his daughters, who immediately became fond of me and started to call me mom. We always had fun together and the girls lent me a helping hand around my home and with my nonprofit events whenever I needed them. He was an entrepreneur with his own business, so he had a flexible schedule. He knew I worked hard, so he always made sure to bring me dinner or cook me dinner after a long day. He was a great cook! I used to call him "the king of barbecue," although he was great at cooking many other things. One day after work, I came home to a surprise. He called me at work earlier that day and told me that as soon as I got home to go out to my back patio. I did just that, and saw that he had turned my patio into a relaxing oasis! He bought me patio furniture, put out tiki torches, a gas grill, and other decor. It was the sweetest gesture I think I had ever received from anyone!

We got engaged after dating for eight months. He was a good man with a very generous heart. In retrospect, our relationship progressed a little too fast. I did not know as much about him as I thought I did. After we got engaged, I was beginning to see a completely different side to him. It was almost as if a switch had flipped. He had some unresolved issues from his childhood, including abandonment. He was treated differently from his brothers and sisters because he had a different father than they did. He was very close with his mother and thought she tried to intentionally leave him when she died from having hip surgery. He also told me his wife left him and cheated on him, leaving him and those three girls behind, which is why they got divorced. I always felt there was more to the story but whenever I would try to get to the bottom of it, he would blow it off and avoid the conversation. He kept all of the details very surface level.

His insecurities started to become more and more evident. The fact that he was twelve years older than me started to bother him. He felt like he wasn't worthy of me and often asked me what I saw in him and why I chose to be with him. I never looked at his age as an issue. I was more concerned about his heart and his spirit than his age. He started to become controlling whenever we weren't together. He wanted to monitor my every move. He often blew up my phone and accused me of seeing someone else or cheating when I wasn't able to answer right away. He made me so furious I told him, "Do I need to create a timecard and clock in and out with you?" Our relationship was quickly becoming toxic and tumultuous. The arguing became intense. What happened to the sweet, gentle, loving, free-spirited man I fell in love with that was so sweet to my parents? His communication was horrible. Whenever I brought up an issue that we needed to talk about, he got up and left. He was never mature enough to handle conflict. He was an avoider, which frustrated me to no end. I was tired of being the adult when it came to handling the difficult issues in the relationship.

I will never forget one particular incident in which he acted completely out of character, so much so that it scared me. We were at our favorite hangout spot listening to live music and having cocktails and food as usual. We always met up with mutual friends there. One night, a male mutual friend was getting ready to leave, gave me a hug, which I didn't think anything of, then gave me a quick kiss on the cheek. Ten minutes later, my fiancé was on the other side of the bar fighting this guy and even opened the door with his head, dragging him outside. It was awful. I was so embarrassed because I viewed the cheek kiss and hug as innocent. I had no feelings whatsoever for this guy and he really didn't mean anything by it. I didn't know how I could ever show my face in the restaurant again, especially since I had planned to have my nonprofit launch event there.

Once I saw that side of him, I should have put a nail in the coffin of the relationship. I get that he saw it as the guy disrespecting him, but at the same time there was a much better way of handling the situation than acting like a *thug* in the club. My favorite hangout spot was now ruined because of his insecurities. Countless times I told him, "I am with you because I want to be with you. If I wanted somebody else, I would be with somebody else." That went in one ear and out the other. Low self-esteem is a beast!

I threatened to leave him several times, but each time he said he would change. He would get better for a little while, then go back to the same old shenanigans. When we were good, we were really good. When we were bad, we were really bad. The girls were never an issue in the relationship, but his insecurities were damaging to our overall dynamics.

I suggested we go to counseling, not necessarily for me, but so he could get over his past and stop projecting his anger on me. He refused to go to counseling to address his toxic behaviors. I was doing everything I knew possible to try to make the relationship work because I truly loved him, flaws and all.

Between me trying to stay financially afloat with my new business and working my butt off with contract work, seeing clients, attending numerous networking events, and doing my nonprofit work, the stress of the relationship was too much. I loved him but also loved myself and peace even more. He always made excuses not to change. He toyed with the idea of us starting a smokehouse restaurant together. I tried to encourage him to capitalize off being such a talented cook. With the way our relationship was, there was no way I could run a business with this fool! I think he was bipolar but undiagnosed. He was severely draining me emotionally and spiritually.

I went to my energy healer for a reset. She lived a few miles from my house. She was a petite Indonesian reverend who was well versed in a variety of religions and religious practices. She also happened to be a psychic medium. As soon as I walked into her room and sat down, she said, "I feel like you want to burst into tears any minute. Your heart is so sad." She was right. I wanted to scream and cry. I told her about the issue I was having with my fiancé.

"He is not the one for you," she said. "But you have to decide if you will choose him over yourself and your peace of mind."

She was right. I had a decision to make.

She asked me if I had ever had a past life reading.

"A past life what?" I asked. I had never heard of it but was curious to learn more. She said that my fiancé and I had met in a past life. He was a fifty-eight-year-old man who had suffered heartbreak. He also suffered from lung issues, something similar to emphysema.

In our past life, we met as I was doing community service. My duties caused me to leave town, and I left him before he had a chance to express his love for me. Hmmm, it made sense because he had abandonment issues and thought that I was going to leave him for someone else. She also saw me lying on a table in peasant's clothing. There were people standing around me, who took my heart out of my body, offered it as a sacrifice to God, then placed my heart back inside my body. When I got up from the table afterward, I looked like a priestess. I had on an elaborate headdress and a robe of silver, white, and gold with bright light all around me. As I proceeded through the session and she completed her energy work, she told me that she released a heavy energy from my back. She said she felt that it was my fiancé trying to control me from behind.

She also told me that when your soul elevates or tries to elevate, the negative energy tries to suck you back in to keep you from moving forward. Man, did I have a lot to process and think about. Even though the past life reading was something I had never experienced, it did confirm some things for me in terms of his behaviors and why I have such a huge heart to help and serve others.

As much as I tried to hold on and make things work, enough was enough. He brought the absolute worst out in me. I didn't recognize who I was anymore. I was so angry and resentful. I broke off the engagement. I gave back that beautiful sapphire and diamond engagement ring. Everything else he ever gave me I put it in a box and dropped it off on his front porch. I wanted nothing else to do with him, ever! I didn't want to see him or have reminders of him around me. I didn't even want to be his friend. We were planning to have a destination wedding and get married in Fiji. We were going to elope in October 2019. So much for that. I'm so glad I dodged that bullet. Even though I had already purchased a beautiful blush-colored, mermaid-style wedding dress and matching veil, I was done. I no longer cared. I donated the dress to an organization called "Brides Against Breast Cancer." I figured someone could find joy and happiness in the dress that I would never get to wear. If his wife truly did leave him, I could see why. If he was treating me horribly, I could only imagine what she went through. I cut him off completely. The most hurtful part was having to cut the girls off too. I did not want him to try to use them to weasel his way back to me. That part still hurts, even as I'm writing this right now. The major lessons I learned with this relationship were that I can love somebody else's children as if they were my own but that I cannot love somebody into wholeness, no matter how much I tried. They have to want to help themselves. Darkness attracts light, so be very aware of who you let get close to you. Not everybody is seeking healing. Nevertheless, he did plant the seed for me to start my own physical therapy business, so the pain I endured in this relationship was not all in vain.

I have been told multiple times that I have the "gift of goodbye." When I feel that something or someone no longer serves its or their purpose, I do not have a hard time letting go, and, when I do, there is a calmness in my spirit confirming to me that I made the right decision. Do I second guess myself at times? Yes, of course! However, when I center myself back on my core values and beliefs, I once again have confirmation that I made the right decision. Numerous times I have had female family members and friends vent to me about relationships and men that they are confused about or keep going back to once the relationship has ended. They tell me, "Girl, I wish I was like you. You have no trouble cutting people off or letting something go if it's not working for you."

I tell them, "I love myself too much to allow negative energy into my circle, to carry dead weight, to put effort into people who don't put the same effort into me, to entertain people who do not see my worth, or to continue to deal with those who I perceive are not genuine and have ulterior motives."

I still posed the following question to myself: "Why was I so successful at my career and not successful at love?" Even though I did not understand, I had to go with it. As I pondered this, I stumbled upon a quote that summed things up: "Your mate comes when you are operating in your purpose. You won't miss them." I had to roll with it. In the meantime, I still had a purpose to fulfill.

*12*

---

## Developing Patience Through My Patients

I HAVE ALWAYS CONSIDERED MY JOB AS A PHYSICAL therapist as a form of worship. April 10, 2016, as I sat in church, the minister said, "Worship has many expressions. Anything you do for God's glory is worship." I have met countless patients who are Christians or people of strong faith. I mentioned before the experience I had leaving my full-time job for another job, only to return to my original job. It was revealed to me at that time that it was not about the money or recognition, but my job was truly a ministry. It was my expression of worship.

One day at work I was in the supply room grabbing socks for a patient. One of the patient care technicians entered the room and we began chatting. She randomly told me about a video she saw of a woman in the Philippines who was about to have her leg amputated and would die from the infection because the leg was black with gangrene. She prayed to God for a second chance and if she received that chance, she would dedicate her life to spreading the gospel. The woman went to a preacher of her faith who prayed over her and there was visual proof that the circulation was restored to her leg. The patient care technician said, "I believe in miracles and, boy, does God perform miracles." She often confided in me about the pain she had in her feet from plantar fasciitis and I would advise her. This day, she said, "I just want to be healed." I told her she would be healed because she had faith and that she was already taking the first step by setting up her physical therapy appointment. She also said to me, "You will make so much money doing your own thing!"

People constantly asked me if I considered starting my own practice, but I always shunned the idea. It's too much competition, too much work, too much of a headache, and I didn't want to deal with the reimbursement shenanigans of the insurance companies. I always said it's not about the money but about God working through me to help heal his people.

About two years prior, I had a patient who I became very close with. She viewed me as a daughter and even confided in me things she would not even tell her own family. One day, her biological daughter was visiting her in the hospital and randomly said to me, "I see you having your own practice. God wanted me to tell you that."

"I have not yet been led to do that," I said. "But I am not counting it out." Once again, I cringed at the responsibility associated with having my own practice, but I did not totally shut out the possibility.

In 2012, I came home from work one day and lay on my couch. I had a long day and was exhausted. I noticed earlier that day my left leg felt numb, but I associated it with exercising and lifting patients. I fell asleep but was awakened a few hours later by a sensation of numbness on the left side of my face. I had a slight headache but attributed it to fatigue and allergies. I went upstairs to bed and went back to sleep. Upon waking the next morning, the left side of my face was still numb in addition to my tongue, lips, left arm, and my left leg. I was panicking. I knew all the signs and symptoms of a stroke. I could speak, and I did not have facial or arm droop. However, I knew something was not right. I was scheduled to work that day. I called and stated I was having symptoms and was on my way to the emergency room. As I was driving, I felt like my symptoms were getting worse and worse. I called my parents and oldest sister to tell them what was happening. I was in a panic. I told them I would call them back and keep them posted. When I arrived at the emergency room, I told the person at the front desk the symptoms I was having, and they immediately took me back to an exam room.

My vitals were taken. My heart rate and blood pressure were elevated, but not to alarming levels. It indicated the amount of anxiety I had about the entire situation. The ER doctor came in. He knew who I was because I saw him around the hospital all the time. He asked me, "How did you get to the hospital?"

I told him that I had driven myself. He saw me in my scrubs.

"Were you planning to try to work today?" he asked.

"Yes," I answered.

He told me to hold out my hand, then playfully slapped the back of my hand.

"You know better!" he said. "You know you should have not driven here by yourself with the symptoms that you had."

He was right. I should have gotten help. They initiated a stroke protocol. I was taken to get an MRI of my head. After the MRI, the ER doctor came back and said, "We need to keep you overnight for observation." Normally patients for medical observation were put on the third floor of the hospital, but to help maintain my privacy as an employee, they graciously put me on the fourth floor in a large corner room. All of the rooms were private.

I called my family to update them on what was going on. They drove up from White Plains to see me. I was kept overnight in the hospital and did not get any rest. Between getting up constantly to use the bathroom from all of the IV fluids and medicine being pumped into me and the nurse tech coming every two hours to check my vitals, I got no sleep whatsoever. Later that night, a neurologist came to my room and did an exam. He reviewed my MRI and explained that I had areas of enhanced foci in the brain upon imaging. He said that those areas were consistent with a migraine diagnosis. He stated that I had atypical migraines given the numbness I was having with my symptoms. He wanted me to have another brain MRI with contrast and come back to see him as an outpatient. Migraines, huh? I was relieved that I didn't have a stroke.

About two months after my migraine diagnosis, I received an order to work with a patient who was having stroke-like symptoms. Upon entering the patient's room to complete the initial evaluation, I questioned her about the symptoms she was having. She said that she had a slight headache and that the whole left side of her body was numb. There was no interruption in her speech and no weakness on the left side of her body. She was still able to walk. She told me that one doctor that had examined her told her that nothing was wrong with her and that she had conversion disorder and was "pretending." Conversion disorder is when someone experiences a lot of mental stress and it manifests as physical symptoms in the body without a medical explanation for the symptoms. She was very distraught about the situation, so I shared with her my experience I had.

"Really?" she said. She questioned me further about the testing I had done and how I was currently feeling. I shared all of the information with her. I saw a glimmer of hope in her eyes that everything was going to be fine. I reassured her that she would be okay. She graciously thanked me for sharing my experience with her. Her MRI results showed that she also had areas of increased foci in the brain, which was indicative of migraines. God quickly used what I deemed a scary experience to help my patient.

I recall another patient who was admitted to the hospital and had a cancer diagnosis. She was having trouble with her short-term memory and difficulty with her speech and finding the right words. She was also receiving chemotherapy at the time. The doctors had run multiple tests on her, mostly to determine if she had a stroke or some other brain abnormalities. Her scans were all clear. The doctors diagnosed her with conversion disorder. She was very upset that she was basically being told that she was "crazy." I asked her if she had noticed changes in her memory and speech since she started chemotherapy. Her face lit up.

"As a matter of fact, yes," she said. "After my third round, I began to notice some changes and it has only gotten worse."

At the time I was in the process of developing a cancer rehab program and had learned about a condition known as chemo brain or chemo fog. I discussed this condition with her. I informed her that chemotherapy can cause thinking and memory problems to occur during and after cancer treatment. Chemo brain can also be called cancer-related cognitive impairment or cognitive dysfunction. Chemo brain symptoms may include decreased short-term memory, problems finding words, short attention span, and difficulty concentrating and multitasking. My patient was exhibiting all of these symptoms. She thanked me and said that she would discuss this further with her oncologist. I advised her to have her oncologist refer her to a speech and language pathologist to help with her cognitive function. I asked her further questions about her career and found out that she worked in special education as a specialist. She loved her job. I told her that my oldest sister worked in special education and was on the fence about transitioning to a new position as a specialist. Actually, my sister was quite stressed out about that decision. My patient described her career path, which was identical to my sister's. She further confirmed some things that I was able to pass along to my sister to help her with her decision. I blessed my patient with information and, in turn, was blessed back immediately to be able to help my sister!

I ENCOUNTERED ANOTHER patient who had been diagnosed with stage-four colon cancer. For some reason during our treatment session, he asked me "Are you a Christian? Do you believe in God?" I told him that I was and how I believed that God could heal you from anything if you have faith and believe. He went on to say, "I knew you were a Christian by the positive energy and the smile you gave me when you came in." Normally I avoid religious conversations at work to remain culturally sensitive to everyone, but when a patient starts telling me about the goodness of God, I can't bite my tongue. I have to speak on it. The patient went on to tell me how he prayed and took communion for healing while he was receiving chemotherapy. He stated after he completed chemo and went to have another scan and that the only cancer left was a tumor in the colon that had to removed. There was no other evidence of metastatic disease anywhere in his body. He began to cry and praise God. I grabbed his hand and asked if I could pray with him. He agreed. All I know is, the power of prayer, faith, and communion is real!

ONE OF THE very first lymphedema patients I treated had breast cancer and a history of lymphedema. She also had an anxiety disorder and often felt claustrophobic in certain environments. She told me that she had PTSD from her breast cancer treatment. Being a new lymphedema therapist, when she walked into my treatment room, she immediately told me how "cramped" the room was and that the room felt claustrophobic. I was thankful to even be able to have a space to do my lymphedema treatment. I knew then that it was going to be a challenge to treat her. Part of lymphedema treatment is having to have the swollen extremity bandaged to reduce swelling. At first, she refused the bandages because she did not want to feel confined. How was I supposed to treat her and do what was best? Eventually, she complied. We had numerous conversations about her experience with breast cancer and her lymphedema.

"You just have the right touch," she said. "It's like you were born to do this."

I told her that I felt that this was my ministry.

She teared up and said, "It is such a blessing for you to be so young [34] and already know what your purpose is in life."

I TREATED A forty-two-year-old woman with breast cancer who had a double mastectomy with TRAM flap reconstruction. She also seemed to have PTSD from her cancer treatment. She always brought her twelve-year-old daughter with her to the therapy sessions. It was amazing how we were able to talk about God and faith during our sessions. I served on the host committee for a Susan G. Komen Greater Atlanta fundraising event for breast cancer research. I had an extra ticket to the event and God placed it on my heart to invite her. She gladly accepted the invitation. She looked beautiful the night of the event! She mentioned how she had never been to an event of that magnitude and how special it made her feel. We ate, laughed, danced, and, most of all, she was able to be among other breast cancer survivors and other people who were supporters of breast cancer research. She was thankful and told me that attending the event renewed her self-confidence. That made my heart smile more than anything.

I VERY FONDLY recall working with a fifty-five-year-old Black man with prostate cancer. His cancer had returned. He had a wife of twenty years and two teenage children. He had just started a new medication. He also had metastasis to his lungs. He developed lymphedema in both legs and also swelling of the genitals. He was frustrated that it was affecting his ability to walk and use the bathroom properly in addition to not being able to be intimate with his wife. Despite all that he was going through, he was still working full-time as a pharmaceutical sales rep. During our treatment sessions, I tried to keep the conversation light and talk to him about anything other than cancer. We often talked about our favorite movies as he was a huge movie buff. He was usually very talkative and outgoing during his physical therapy sessions with me, however, during one particular session, he was unusually quiet. I asked him what was wrong because I could feel that he was not himself and could tell that he had a lot on his mind.

"With everything that's going on with me," he said, "I just want to make sure I am prepared and leaving my family in a good situation if something were to ever happen to me and I don't survive this cancer."

I assured him that the fact that he was doing everything he could to stay healthy was him taking the necessary steps to leave his family in a good situation. His wife attended a treatment session with him, and I taught her how to bandage his legs to help with the swelling. After about four to six weeks of intense treatment, his legs returned to normal size, and his genital swelling was completely gone. He was ecstatic. He was so amazed at how quickly I was able to help him after being told by some doctors that there was nothing else that could be done for him. He advocated for himself and insisted that his doctor refer him to me.

He wrote me a beautiful thank you card that read, "Crystal, just a small token of my appreciation. I am very grateful for all you have done to get me back on my feet. You are a gift from God! Thank you so very much!"

Inside the card was a pair of movie tickets.

"Take some time off from your hard work and go enjoy your favorite movie!" he wrote on the other side of the card. Once again, this patient encounter served as validation that my job was my ministry and my purpose.

ABOUT A YEAR later, after I had left my job and started my nonprofit and physical therapy business, a former patient/nurse reached out to me. She was a breast cancer survivor and I treated her for breast cancer rehab. We often had very candid conversations. She was very hard on herself since she was a nurse with a husband who was a surgeon and did not realize she had stage-two breast cancer. She had to undergo surgery, chemo, and radiation. She often said, "Crystal, I should have known better, I work in the medical field, and I just should have known!" The first time she made that statement she cried uncontrollably. I sat on the treatment table next to her to console her. She said she had a friend whose husband passed away from cancer and had some items that she wanted to donate to an organization. I informed her that my nonprofit would gladly accept the items. I made arrangements to pick up the items from her at her home. Upon arrival, she looked great! She was so excited that her hair had grown back and that she had completed all of her treatments. The items consisted of lozenges to help with nausea associated with chemo, masks, oral care products, nutritional drinks, bed pads, and a lymphedema pump for the lower body. I gratefully loaded the items in my car and headed home. Once I got the items inside my home, I began organizing them and taking inventory of what I had received. One item caught my attention. There was a bottle of prescription medication that was in the box, and it had the name of the person that the items belonged to. My mouth dropped wide open. Shortly after the tears started to roll. The donated items I received were from a former patient who I treated for lymphedema associated with prostate cancer. This was the same patient who gave me a beautiful thank you card with movie tickets inside. It is amazing how things come full circle. I gave to him the gift of healing, and he in turn in his death gave a gift to me of items needed by my nonprofit organization. God truly has a unique way of reminding you that you are indeed on the correct path, even when you doubt yourself.

I RECONNECTED WITH an associate I met through a mutual friend at a birthday party. She was thirty-nine years old, an elementary school teacher, and a single mother of a ten-year-old son. Within two months of reconnecting with her, she passed away. Another loss. Why did I reconnect with her? Why did God allow our paths to cross again? I met her in 2011. She was cool but after meeting her, we were only friends on social media. We never really hung out or talked personally on the phone. Even on social media, there was not much more than a status like or comment here or there. I found out that she had been diagnosed with breast cancer. She won her first battle with breast cancer and was cancer free for about two to three years. I kept up with her on social media and saw her do marathons and continue to work out at the gym.

I arrived at work at the hospital one day, a little later than usual. Normally, I assist with creating the patient schedule for the day, but due to being late, my schedule was already set. As I wrote down my patient list, I saw a familiar name. A lot of patients tend to return to the hospital and many names are familiar anyway. Little did I know that patient was my friend from social media. She immediately recognized me when I entered her room. She was excited to see me and said, "It feels so good to see a familiar face while I'm dealing with all of this." I was saddened to learn that her cancer had returned and had spread to her liver. She was also having complications from her chemotherapy. After she was discharged from the hospital, I reached out to her not only as her therapist but as a friend. We exchanged numbers and I told her to call me if she needed *anything*. A few weeks later, my words were put to the test. She called me to take her to pick up her medications from the pharmacy because she didn't have the energy to drive. At the time I was in downtown Atlanta, shadowing a therapist at a lymphedema clinic. It just so happened that I was only there for half of the day, so I had the perfect opportunity to help her. Within one hour of her call, I was at her home. I had to assist her in walking because she was swollen in her abdomen and both her legs and in pain. There was no way she could have driven. She was experiencing shortness of breath by just talking to me. I told her, "You don't have to talk, just rest." I assisted her several times by picking her up from her chemotherapy appointments and taking her home because she was receiving treatment at the hospital where I worked. There were days where I had to physically help her lift her legs to get in the car as well as help her up the stairs in her home. I also made sure she had food before I dropped her off. Two months after reconnecting with her, I was informed by her sister that she was put on home hospice care, on the day of her birthday. I continued to check in on her. Two weeks later she passed. At the end of the same week, I had a dream about her. I could see her with her scarf on her head and her sweatpants, which was the last thing I remember seeing her wear. She kissed me on my cheek and thanked me for helping her in my dream. Who knew that when we first met, I would be a person that she needed as she was fighting for her life.

IN A SHORT time, I met four female patients who I deem very special to me. One of them was a lymphedema patient who came to me very frustrated. She had been to many other therapists without successful treatment of her condition. She had pain and swelling in both legs since the age of ten. She had recently moved from Birmingham, Alabama, with her husband and said that she did not have successful treatment there or when she moved to

Atlanta. It was difficult for her to wear shoes and her legs were in pain when she walked and stood. She was forced to wear larger pants to accommodate her swollen legs. She said she did an internet search and found the clinic where I was located. She had a friendly spirit, and we quickly connected like girlfriends that had known each other for a long time. With subsequent treatment, her leg swelling significantly improved and she was finally able to wear jeans and shoes that she had not been able to wear in ages. She was very grateful.

We bonded during treatment and began to hang out together once her treatment was completed. We developed a wonderful relationship. Even now, we are like sisters and the best of friends. She reminded me of my oldest sister. I could talk to her about anything! I informed her that I was working on forming a nonprofit to help support cancer patients. Without hesitation she told me she would help. Her mom passed away from breast cancer, so the cause was near and dear to her heart.

Shortly after, I met three other breast cancer patients. The first one was telling me how she wanted to write a book about her breast cancer journey. She was very physically active and passionate about physical fitness and helping others. She was still in the process of getting breast reconstruction. She was in her last phase and was scheduled to have nipple tattooing within a few weeks of me treating her. After she received the nipple tattooing, she came to me in tears. The tattoo ink faded immediately, and she had paid over $700 to have it done. She was on a fixed income and financially could not afford to pay to have the work redone. She was told by the tattoo artist, "This happens sometimes, unfortunately. I can't predict when the ink will or won't take." We were both dumbfounded by that statement. It's a shame that people try to pad their pockets from patients fighting cancer who are already financially strained.

The second breast cancer patient turned out to be my sorority sister! We were in the same local chapter and didn't even know it because the chapter was so large. I knew her name was familiar, then it dawned on me that her name was listed in the newsletter for prayer due to having breast cancer treatment. She was interested in helping others with cancer and their nutritional needs through healthy eating and detoxing as she felt that this was not stressed enough during her own journey.

The third patient I encountered had stage-four metastatic breast cancer. I treated her for twelve weeks. She was a classy and sophisticated Black woman, very well-spoken. She was the same age as my mom and reminded me of her. Her husband would bring her to her therapy appointments, and they drove almost fifty miles each way to come and see me for treatment. We were the only facility that accepted her insurance plan at the time. I was treating her for lymphedema in her right arm. She had not had any surgery for breast cancer but was on chemotherapy to try to shrink her tumors. The cancer had eaten away at her right breast, and you could see scarring where it had damaged her skin. I had never seen a breast cancer case this severe. She was a God-fearing, spiritual woman. She shared with me her testimony about her treatments. I later found out she was actually a minister. She told me how she had cancer in her lungs and bones, however, on her last scans, there was no longer any evidence. She also shared with me how the hospital where she received treatment canceled over $67,000 in medical debt for her. I was in awe of her strength and everything she had endured as she continued to fight breast cancer daily. I encouraged her to write a book about her experience so that other people would be blessed through her story and told her she should title it "Faith through Survivorship." She shied away from the idea. Our treatment sessions consisted of us talking, praying, and often crying. We poured into each other in indescribable ways. One day she said, "You are doing great work, but you need God to open the door for you for a larger platform for you to help others." She confirmed many other things for me that I was currently in the process of developing. As we were sitting in my small lymphedema treatment room, she looked around and said, "You are a strong believer, and you are too boxed in where you are right now to be able to have the reach you need to have to help other people." I knew she was right. I felt that I was operating in my calling and purpose by doing my current work with lymphedema and cancer patients, but I still felt like something was missing. I felt that I had a greater calling. It was put in my spirit to develop a different way to help cancer patients.

I was reminded of a conversation I had with a colleague.

As I was in the process of developing a post-operative mastectomy protocol for my facility, I spoke with a nurse for one of the plastic surgeons at the facility who performed breast reconstruction surgery for women who have had mastectomies due to breast cancer. We began talking about the lack of resources in the area and how a facility was needed that encompassed physical therapy, lymphedema treatment, nutrition, wellness, exercise, etc. for patients so they don't have to go to multiple places to receive care. I heard my patients say to me countless times that once their cancer treatment was completed, they felt like they had been "dumped off" to fend for themselves. They were left emotionally and spiritually broken in addition to having to deal with physical side effects, which led them to have a decreased quality of life. That was it! Cancer patients needed a holistic approach to their care. It's not just about their cancer diagnoses. It is about restoration!

I told these last four patients about my desire to start a nonprofit to help all cancer survivors and they were all on board. Little did I know that these four ladies, who were my patients and all breast cancer survivors, would become board members for my nonprofit organization. The Champions Can! Foundation was launched and officially formed on April 6, 2017.

The organization's mission was penned as follows: Champions Can! Foundation for Cancer Wellness, Inc. is a 501(c)(3) nonprofit organization that advocates for cancer survivorship by striving to provide services to unite, support, and educate individuals before during, and after their course of cancer treatment with the goal of promoting cancer survivorship and improving quality of life, regardless of the cancer diagnosis.

The organization's purpose was developed as follows: Champions Can! Foundation for Cancer Wellness, Inc. offers a comprehensive cancer wellness program with a holistic approach to overall wellness that will provide and achieve the following:

- Restoration of physical functioning through the promotion of physical fitness and physical activity.
- Restoration of psychological/spiritual well-being through counseling, chaplaincy, energy healing, meditation, etc.
- Promotion of healthy eating and nutritional counseling to aid in physical healing.
- Coordination and referral of other community resources per individual need.
- Community education regarding cancer care and post-cancer care, cancer survivorship, and cancer recovery.
- Improvement of self-esteem through improving physical appearance and referrals to appropriate resources.
- Support of cancer survivors and their families through the recovery process.
- Evidence-based research and backing for services that are offered.

With the foundation's mission defined, Champions Can! was born and began charging forward to change the lives of cancer patients for the better!

## 13

## Illogical Logic

EVERYTHING IN MY CAREER WAS GOING WELL. THE lymphedema program that I started was finally well established. We were bursting at the seams with new referrals to the point we had a four-week waiting list for new patient evaluations and the other certified lymphedema therapist at the clinic shifted from doing full-time orthopedic physical therapy to doing full-time lymphedema treatment. I had many speaking engagements at my organization regarding lymphedema and breast cancer rehabilitation. I also helped facilitate patient simulation labs for Doctor of Physical Therapy students. I was asked by physicians to speak at events throughout the healthcare system. I was becoming well known for my lymphedema expertise. Life was good. I was also in the process of planning the first launch event for my nonprofit organization. I was comfortable, financially secure, happy, and, at the time, I was also in a beautiful relationship with a man who simply adored me.

One day, I felt like I was blindsided at work by my supervisor and my department director because they felt that I was "gossiping" when, in actuality, I was having a personal private conversation with another coworker who I often confided in. My supervisor walked in on the conversation, and my colleague and I stopped our conversation. Later that afternoon, she stopped my colleague outside and asked her, "What were you and Crystal talking about? It looked like you were gossiping." Really? Are we in high school?

Within the same two weeks, another colleague and I (a compression garment fitter who was crucial to the success of my program who I had also befriended) were having a private conversation. She was having a difficult time with a situation regarding a customer and was asking my opinion. The other lymphedema therapist at the clinic—the clinic supervisor—felt that something that was said was in reference to her (which was untrue), so she approached me and asked, "Do you have a problem with me?" I told her I did not, which was true, but she still seemed to think that I disliked her. I am the type of person that when it comes to my work, I am very focused and I do not make a lot of time for small talk. I started the lymphedema program, and a lot of work went into it, which included managing a full patient load, all documentation, answering questions and assisting colleagues, continued program planning, and planning for students and other speaking engagements, not to mention also being consumed with getting my nonprofit up and running.

I went to Phoenix, Arizona, to begin working on my Advanced Lymphedema Management certification. I was out of the office for seven days. Upon my return, I began catching up on my work emails. I saw an email thread going around about teamwork, respect, and "avoiding workplace gossip." I rolled my eyes as I continued to read the email. I saw a notification on my calendar that my department director and clinic supervisor both wanted to meet with me. I immediately had a bad feeling in my gut about the whole situation. As I walked into the boardroom, my supervisor and director were both sitting at the table. My supervisor spoke first. I listened and took notes to be sure I understood what she was trying to say, which in my opinion revealed a load of insecurities that she had. Then my director chimed in with a book quote and told me that my supervisor was experiencing "incivility in the workplace" because of me. She said that she wished that I would treat her the same way that I treated my patients. Say what! I was appalled. I am who I am. I have never been told that I was unapproachable or unprofessional by any of my colleagues or patients. I even received an employee of the month award and numerous compliments. I felt that they were attacking my character. I had worked for this organization for almost ten years. Many of my colleagues confided in me because they felt that I gave them honest guidance and advice and also because they know that they could trust me. As I went back to work after the meeting, my mind and spirit were disturbed for the rest of the day. After work, I sat in my car and thought, "Lord, why? I am a good person. I don't deserve this." I was frustrated and wanted to cry. I was then reminded of a sermon by Joel Osteen, one of my favorite speakers, whom I listened to faithfully on satellite radio. He said, "when things are being stirred up, God is shifting things around." I distinctly heard a voice that said, "It's time to move." *Huh? No, that can't be right.* I heard it again. "It is time to move. The longer you stay here, the more comfortable you will become, and you will limit yourself and what God has planned for you." Although it did not make sense to me, I felt an overwhelming sense of peace about what I heard.

Then my mind kicked into high gear. Leave my job? But I make good money! My program is doing well and getting lots of referrals. I am serving my purpose there and helping people with cancer and lymphedema, which I am very passionate about. Financially, I am not ready to make this move. The timing isn't right. I need to work full time, and I need to have steady income. I left my organization full time before, in pursuit of a new project that didn't work out. I don't want to be in that uncomfortable place again! I came up with every reason to fight the voice that I heard. Then this was put in my spirit: "God will not lead you where He will not sustain you. The time is now." I continued to ponder the day's events. Leaving my job right now just didn't make sense! I had established a name for myself. My patients loved me. My program was successful. I was not married, and although I was in a relationship, I did not want to have to lean on him financially if needed. This was then dropped in my spirit: "The Lord made the earth and the fullness thereof. Ask and you will receive." I was also reminded of a saying by comedian and talk show host Steve Harvey. "Just jump! You may get scratched up, bumped, and bruised along the way, but just jump! You never know your full potential unless you just jump!" I sighed, pulled out of the parking lot, and headed home.

I went home and prayed about it. After thinking, I said to myself, "Crystal, you don't want to make a decision just based on emotion. You can't run from a situation just because you are being challenged, because you are being put under pressure, or because things are getting hard." The voice came to me over and over again: "It is time to move." As frightened as I was, I drafted a resignation letter. Was I really doing this? Was I leaving my security? "God, I trust you, even though this does not make sense to me right now, I know it will eventually," I said. God's thoughts were not my thoughts, and His ways were not my ways. "Crystal, you have to have faith and just be obedient."

I went to bed and felt a sense of peace even though it was still in my mind: *This doesn't make sense but okay. God, let your will be done.* I woke up the next morning, no change of heart and no second-guessing. I entered my workplace, bright and cheerful and greeted everyone. After a while, I went to my clinic supervisor and asked to speak with her. I gave her the resignation letter and told her that I would remain in my position for another month to ensure a seamless transition for the program.

"I am so sorry to hear this, and I apologize if I had anything to do with your decision," she said.

BINGO. She knew she was wrong, but at that time, I really wanted to thank her because had it not been for her actions, I would not have had the courage to step out on faith. I once heard that, "God will use your adversaries and people who are against you to promote you and propel you into your destiny!" This was more confirmation for my next move.

## 14

## Accolades, Applause, and a Pause

THE YEAR OF 2019 WAS MY FIRST FULL YEAR BEING ON my own career-wise. Although I was previously working for another organization, I had already begun the process of working on my own practice, Eminence Physical Therapy. Once I left the organization, I had to step everything up a notch, being that I was forced to fly solo sooner than I anticipated. I worked hard to get my name out there for Eminence Physical Therapy. I did *tons* of networking and attended events, health fairs, and speaking engagements. It was also a very busy year for my nonprofit organization Champions Can! Foundation for Cancer Wellness, Inc. I was continuing to lay the foundation for my projects and was feeling very good about it, even though I was working very hard. The stress was intense, yet I felt free that I was working for myself, making my own schedule, and playing by my own rules.

I decided to keep my business mobile to avoid overhead costs because it was a new business. I wanted to keep my operating expenses low. Just as I was becoming comfortable with my business model, I met someone who presented me with an opportunity I could not refuse. I went to a continuing-education networking event for a contract company I was also working for. I saw some of my former colleagues and everyone wanted to know how my business was going. I was prepared and able to give everyone folders and marketing materials I had created. One colleague told me, "You are fearless, and I always admired your drive." As I continued to work my way around the room, I overheard a conversation at the table next to me. The woman was a massage therapist and had her own business. She was also a certified lymphedema therapist and had a lymphedema clinic inside her massage therapy practice. She had hired an occupational therapist who was lymphedema certified and was doing all of the lymphedema treatments and also had a compression garment shop and garment fitter. Her business model was very similar to mine being that she did not accept insurance and services were cash only. She was unable to sustain the salary of her lymphedema therapist and had to let her go. The owner was now forced to do the lymphedema treatments on her own, in which she preferred not to do and was currently looking for help.

I chimed in and introduced myself and told her who I was and about my private practice. She asked me if I was looking for a clinic space for my business. I told her I was mobile but was interested to see the space she had available. She told me, "I really need help! I feel it would be great if you offered your services in my building." She extended an invitation to me to come and see the space. I went home that evening and pondered the idea, but I was still hesitant to take on overhead expenses.

I ended up going to the clinic to view the space. It was beautiful! It was also not very far from my home, and I felt that the location was perfect for me to see patients in the clinic as well as provide mobile visits in the same vicinity. It was a no-brainer. I decided to accept her offer. I began working in the office space in February 2019. This really turned out to be a blessing in disguise because the massage therapist became a referral source for patients. I was actually seeing more patients in clinic than mobile!

It was a wonderful 2019 for my nonprofit organization. We were doing various things in the community and our schedule was full. We were passionate to help and serve our community. We united other cancer survivors as they navigated their journeys. We strived to advocate for cancer survivors and their families for services needed before, during, and after cancer care. We educated our community about the importance of cancer awareness and cancer survivorship. Last but not least, we helped to restore hope to cancer survivors to help them *survive* and live a better quality of life!

Events focused on wholistic wellness, fitness, and lymphedema awareness. We held a retreat, a Caribbean-party fundraiser, set up tables at health fairs, hosted a survivorship day party, and we closed out the year with a breast cancer awareness event.

In the middle of our year of planning, which was around July 2019, I had given the board members different assignments to assist with one particular event that was to take place later in the year. My vice president sent me an email in which I noticed she seemed to be confused about the task that was given to her. I thought to myself, "I had better call her to give more clarification." Upon calling her, I noticed that it was taking her a long time to get her words out and she seemed to be talking in circles. I was overcome with worry and concern. I began asking her a series of questions. She was unable to tell me her address, the day of the week, and was unable to tell me if her husband was at home with her. I remember her telling me that she had developed heart damage and a condition called atrial fibrillation from chemotherapy. Atrial fibrillation is a condition that can lead to a stroke, so my mind immediately went to the thought that she may have had a stroke. She lived on the other side of Atlanta and there was no way I would be able to get to her quickly in the middle of rush hour traffic. I kept searching and trying to call numbers for the emergency medical services closest to her. I still don't know how, but I was able to get to the 911 operator in her county to dispatch help to her.

She was rushed to the local hospital, then subsequently transferred to another specialty hospital the next day. My secretary and I called around to practically every hospital in

Atlanta to find out where she was located. Once we did, we went to see her. As I was in the room, the neurologist came in. I explained to him that I was her friend and physical therapist. He told me that she was given a CAT scan of her brain and it showed that she had tumors in her brain, affecting her speech area. Lord have mercy! Her breast cancer had metastasized into her brain! She was very confused and had expressive and receptive aphasia. She could understand things a lot easier if they were written down and she could read it. Physically, she was still able to move and walk around without assistance. She was kept in the hospital and received ten sessions of gamma knife radiation to the area of the tumors in her brain.

She jokingly told me how she was sitting in her office chair when five huge men burst into her home, put her in the ambulance, and took her to the hospital.

"I didn't know what was happening!" she said. "Crystal, you are responsible for all of this!"

"Yes, I am responsible for all of the chaos," I answered back.

"You saved my life," she said.

After her radiation, she was released home and had home health care. She was improving, but still had some speech deficits. However, her focus was on Champions Can! and making sure the organization was continuing to move forward in her absence.

In all my diligence and toiling, I received several awards. In October 2019, I received the "40 Under 40 Achievement Award" from both *The Network Journal Magazine* of New York City and *Georgia Trend Magazine* for my hard work in serving cancer patients and their families through my private physical therapy practice and my nonprofit organization. *The Network Journal* is New York's leading Black professional and small-business magazine. *Georgia Trend* honors the state's best and brightest under the age of forty in nonprofits, healthcare, business, and more. These were all awards that someone else nominated me for that I did not see coming! I said to myself, "Okay, God, I am going to ride this wave and see where it takes me." I was also featured in a 2019 Academy Award-qualified documentary, *Inside of My Mysterious*

*Life*, which details the life of two women as they battle a chronic condition called lymphedema. The documentary was four-walled and screened at the historic Laemmle Theater in North Hollywood, California. I was also continuing to do heavy marketing for my business and nonprofit and participated in numerous television and radio interviews.

I attended the Living Beyond Breast Cancer (LBBC) Conference in Philadelphia, Pennsylvania. I went with one of my best friends and another associate, who were both breast cancer survivors. I wanted to attend to expand my knowledge for the breast cancer patients I treated, and I also wanted to be there to support my friends. I was astounded to see so many women who had survived breast cancer, were actively going through breast cancer treatment, and those who were thriving and living with metastatic breast cancer.

The workshops were very informative. I attended two particular workshops that focused on breast reconstruction procedures and another workshop with a focus on the side effects of breast cancer treatments and associated medications. At the end of the workshops, there were several questions asked of the facilitators as it related to physical therapy, lymphedema, and breast cancer rehabilitation. The workshop facilitators consisted of plastic surgeons, a breast nipple tattoo artist, and a cancer survivorship clinic nurse. None of them could answer the specific questions women had about lymphedema and cancer rehab, so I took the mic and chimed in with answers in both workshops. After the workshops ended, women came up to me, asking where I practiced and also asking me personal questions about their care. The nurse from the survivorship clinic also approached me at the end and we had a very pleasant and spiritual conversation. She thanked me for answering questions and also talked about how she viewed her job as a ministry. I felt the same way. We had the same passions about helping cancer patients.

After the conference, I reflected on the information received. I could not get out of my mind how many Black women were in attendance at the conference, yet there was only one Black female speaker at the entire conference. None of the breakout workshop sessions were facilitated by a woman of color. At the conference, I received the information for the director of education for LBBC. I sent her an email thanking them for hosting the conference and for the wealth of knowledge I gained at the conference. I also mentioned that I was a physical therapist and certified lymphedema therapist and noticed that lymphedema and breast cancer rehabilitation was not fully addressed and that I was interested in helping to facilitate a workshop. She agreed and stated that this has been discussed as one of the initiatives moving forward. She asked me to send her video clips of me speaking as well as my biography. I did just that and she agreed to be in touch with me regarding facilitating a session once they decided on dates for the conference in 2020. I was ecstatic! This was once again confirmation from God that I was still on the right path in regards to my purpose of helping people as I often prayed to God to "enlarge my territory" so that I could impact more people.

    I was very busy in 2019 between all the awards ceremonies, conferences, and other breast cancer events that I attended. I kept saying to myself, "Once I slow down at the end of the year, I am going to get all of my doctor appointments in for the year." I saw my primary care doctor. Everything checked out well. I saw my OBGYN. Everything checked out well. Even though I was thirty-eight years old, I was adamant about having a mammogram because I had one the previous year that was normal. Because I work with cancer patients daily, I am very proactive regarding my health and wanted to make sure I was covering all bases. I have a strong history of cancer on my dad's side of the family. I had an aunt, first cousin, and second cousin who all had breast cancer. November 5, 2019, I went in for a routine mammogram. A few days later, I got a call saying I needed to come back for a diagnostic mammogram because new calcifications were seen in my left breast. I was shocked. Just last year I had a mammogram that was clear. How could it change so fast? The earliest appointment I could get for a diagnostic mammogram was December 5, 2019. I had to wait practically a whole month. I was beyond stressed.

December 5 arrived and I, very nervous, went in for the mammogram. At the end, the radiologist came in and talked to me about the results. She even showed me the images so that I could see what she was referring to. She said there were two areas of calcifications in my left breast and by looking at them she could not tell what they were. She also said she felt that they were nothing to be concerned about because most women have calcifications, but she said, "I want to be 100 percent sure. Right now, I'm about 95 percent sure." She wanted me to have a biopsy. Fear took over me. I knew that needing a biopsy meant that those calcifications were suspicious, although she did not directly come out and say it. Even though I was afraid, I stayed positive and kept telling myself over and over, "It will be fine." Besides, I was not having any symptoms. I had no discharge from my nipples, skin changes, inversion of my nipples, and no pain. The only thing I noticed that was different was that around the time of my menstrual cycle, both breasts were more tender than normal, but I drank coffee every morning and attributed the breast soreness to that, as well as getting older and my body undergoing hormonal changes.

The only person I told about the biopsy was my oldest sister and one of my close friends who was a breast cancer survivor and the secretary of my nonprofit foundation. The irony of it all was that she initially was a patient I treated for lymphedema in her legs. However, after agreeing to assist me with my nonprofit, she was diagnosed with breast cancer. I did not want to tell anyone else until I had my results. I did not want to worry the rest of my family unnecessarily. The earliest appointment I could get for a biopsy was December 23. Great. Now I had to go into the Christmas holiday wondering about biopsy results after just spending Thanksgiving worrying about the fact that I had to have a diagnostic mammogram.

December 23 came. It was a cloudy, cold, and rainy day. I went to my appointment alone. Once I was taken back into the imaging room, the gravity of what was about to happen suddenly became very heavy. I was afraid of the aftermath. I was thinking I would be fine. "I'm strong; I've got this" is what I told myself. Once my left breast was placed into the machine, the radiologist injected me with numbing medication and described the process to me. The oncology nurse present in the room held my hand and began talking to me to keep me calm. She could sense my fear, worry, and anxiety. We had a conversation about my career and non-profit, which she found very interesting. She began to tell me about her husband's battle with lymphoma. Even though we were talking, it did not distract me from the pressure I could feel in my breast as well as the loud drilling sound that sounded like my breast would be sucked up into a vacuum cleaner at any second. It was very uncomfortable. Once the procedure was over, the nurse took me into a room, bandaged me up, gave me instructions for post-procedure care, and told me that I would be notified of the biopsy results in a few days but that there may be a delay due to the upcoming Christmas holiday.

After the biopsy, I went to my car and sat in the parking lot. I cried. I was not okay. I felt so alone, so empty. I could not get out of my mind the pain from the needle in my breast to inject a local anesthetic, the pain and pressure from having my breast smashed in multiple directions, the pressure from the needle going in, and the vacuuming/drilling sound. I put my head in my hands and cried some more. Once I calmed down, I called my oldest sister and told her about the biopsy procedure. I told her how scary it was and began to cry again. She kept reassuring me that everything was going to be okay and that I should have asked her to come with me.

"I thought I was going to be fine," I told her.

"I know, sis, but this is different. You have never been through something like this before," she said.

I did not reveal to my mom the fact that I had a biopsy until Christmas Day because I did not want to worry her. Just two weeks prior, she felt a lump on her right breast and was worried about it but had just found out that it was a benign cyst from the mammogram she had a few days before. When I told her about my biopsy and showed her the bandage that was still on the outside of my left breast, she said, "Well, hopefully it's nothing, but if it is something at least you are catching it early and whatever it is can be treated."

Even though she was trying to be reassuring, I quickly became dismissive and said, "It's nothing, we just have to go through the motions to make sure it is nothing." I told her that I was not having any breast pain or other symptoms.

Christmas day was warm, sunny, and beautiful. I spent the day with my parents, oldest sister, brother-in-law, and the family pup, Noah. In the back of my mind, I was still worried sick about my pending biopsy results and the fact that I had not received them. What if this was my last time being normal and not having a cancer diagnosis? If I had cancer, how in the world could I possibly tell my family? Could this be my last Christmas holiday with my normal, natural breasts? I immediately had to put those thoughts out of my head, and enjoy the present, the here and now. Two days after Christmas, I received a call from the breast imaging center from the breast navigator nurse, the same one who held my hand during my biopsy. She told me that the pathologists had to do an additional stain on the slides of the sample they took from me, but I should have the final results in a few more days. The lump in my throat dropped to my stomach. I immediately thought, "An additional stain? That must mean that they see something abnormal!" Worry, fear, and anxiety set in once again. I took several deep breaths and then prayed and said, "God, You did not give me a spirit of fear."

December 31, 2019, a day that I will never forget. It was a day in which I received news that would change my life forever. I was in a complete state of denial, shock, and disbelief as I sat in my car in a parking lot. I was in a twilight zone, a space that I had never experienced before in my life. I couldn't even allow tears to roll down my face. How could this be happening to me? Why did life have to throw me such a curveball right now? All the hard work I had put into my business and nonprofit was finally starting to pay off, and now my life would have to come to a screeching halt. Lord, why this timing? Why this date? Why on New Year's Eve? Now I would be forced to face this horrible memory every year! Lord, what was I being prepared for? Your word says You will never put more on me than I can bear, but the uncertainty and gravity of this heavy moment are too much for me! I knew people looked at me as such a strong, resilient soul, but *come on*! I had helped many others through this same situation, yet I didn't have the words to comfort and encourage myself. Certainly, this could not be how my 2020 was going to start. I am a good person. I have a heart for serving and helping others. What was the purpose of me going through this? Please make it all make sense!

Around four thirty p.m. that day, I was driving home from work and about to stop at the grocery store to pick up items needed to start my detox cleanse for the new year. My phone rang and I recognized the number from the breast imaging center.

"May I speak with Crystal?" the voice said.

"This is Crystal," I answered.

"Is this a good time to talk? This is the nurse navigator and the radiologist from the breast center."

I knew this wasn't going to be good from the tone of voice and the fact that both of them were on the phone together.

"I am driving right now, and I need a minute or two to pull over," I said. I asked them to hold. Once I pulled over into a parking lot, I immediately braced myself. My stomach sank. Deep down I already knew what they were about to tell me.

The radiologist said, "Unfortunately, your biopsy results came back positive for DCIS, ductal carcinoma in-situ, which is stage-zero breast cancer. We need to get you set up with another biopsy of the second area of calcifications in your breast, a breast MRI, and genetic testing as soon as possible."

My mind was reeling. I was still trying to process the fact that I was being told I had breast cancer on New Year's Eve. I could not process what they were telling me. Everything turned into a fog.

"Wait, wait, wait what?" I asked. "I have breast cancer?"

"Yes, Crystal, we are so sorry to have to tell you this, but the good news is that this is very early stage and very treatable."

She proceeded to tell me that having a lumpectomy and radiation was the usual course of treatment for DCIS. My mind flashed back to cancer committee meetings and tumor board conferences that I had attended. I remembered the doctors saying, "If a woman is going to get breast cancer, DCIS is the one to have." I felt my mouth moving but it took a minute for words to come out. They were throwing all of the information at me so fast. All I heard was, "You have breast cancer," and I did not hear any of the available dates being tossed at me to have the other testing done.

I finally managed to say, "The genetic counseling can wait, and you can go ahead and set me up with the other appointments." My mind was still racing with a million thoughts, but I was still in a fog and a state of shock. Was this real? Was this really happening? Surely I couldn't be diagnosed with breast cancer because I was too busy educating and helping others with cancer journeys. Who was I going to tell? My family was going to panic, so I couldn't tell them right now. What was I going to do?

After the phone call ended, my OBGYN had received the results of my biopsy and called me about five minutes after the breast center called me. I pulled my car over again to take the call.

"Crystal, did you just get a phone call from the breast center?" she asked.

"Yes, I did, doc. I was told I have breast cancer."

I had worked with my OBGYN at the hospital, and I also had been seeing her for years, so she knew me quite well.

"Crystal, I am so, so sorry, and the fact that it's New Year's Eve I am even more sorry."

I could hear her voice quivering over the phone. I was still in a daze. Even though I worked with a lot of oncologists and breast surgeons, I respected her opinion and asked her who she would recommend for breast care. She gave me the name of a group and said that she would generate the referral for me.

"They treat breast cancer all day, every day and the patients I have sent to them are all now cancer free," she said.

I thanked her for the information, and she again apologized to me.

Dazed, shocked, afraid, head pounding, foggy, stomach-churning, I still went to the grocery store. I tried to act like nothing happened. I was walking through the store purchasing the items for my detox cleanse. I felt like a zombie. Everything and everybody were a blur. I made it through the checkout line. The cashier was friendly and said to me in a very cheerful voice, "Happy New Year!" In a very dry tone of voice, I said it back to her. I loaded the groceries in my car and headed home. The silence in my house was extremely loud. I placed my groceries on the kitchen counter and stood there in disbelief. It was six p.m. I was supposed to go out for New Year's Eve with my friend. She was going to pick me up at seven thirty p.m.

Ironically, I was supposed to be getting ready to go to a black-tie fundraiser for a nonprofit breast cancer support organization, I Will Survive, Inc. All I really wanted to do was crawl into bed and cry my eyes out, but I said I had to dust myself off and get out of the house to take my mind off of my devastating news. I sat on my couch for a few minutes with my head in my hands. Tears welled up in my eyes, but yet I still did not cry. I said to myself "Crystal, the last thing you need to do is sit in this house all alone thinking about breast cancer." I went upstairs, took a shower, and got dressed for the event.

My friend picked me up as promised at seven thirty p.m. She was a breast cancer survivor and was just over a year out of breast cancer treatment. As I mentioned earlier, she revealed to me that she had breast cancer at a launch event for my nonprofit. It's amazing how she was helping other cancer patients, but at the time she was surrounded by other strong breast cancer survivors who she would need to lean on and draw strength from during her own journey. In route to the event, she asked me if I had received the results of my biopsy. I didn't have the nerve to tell her. I said, "Nope, I haven't heard yet. The holidays have delayed everything." She began to cry and became emotional about her journey and the lingering emotional and psychological effects of dealing with a breast cancer diagnosis. I offered emotional support and encouragement to her to take my mind off of my news. Unbeknownst to her, I now finally understood the emotional and psychological effects of breast cancer that she was referring to, which started when I received my diagnosis just a few hours earlier.

Near the event venue, the streets were beautifully decorated with white Christmas lights. The event was inside an art gallery. As we entered, the decor was black, gold, and pink. There was a photo backdrop with a pink carpet. I smiled and took pictures, all glammed up. I was determined to make the best of the night. I mingled, laughed, sipped champagne, danced as midnight approached. I even tossed a pink balloon back and forth to my friend. I still had not said one word to her about my diagnosis. As the night came to a close, we left the event center and headed home. I thanked her for inviting me to the event. I entered my house, went upstairs, got undressed, and lay in my bed. Once again, the silence was very loud. All I wanted to do was sleep and forget that this day ever happened.

*15*

## Trial and Transition (Vision 2020)

JANUARY 1, 2020—NEW YEAR'S DAY. I WOKE UP AROUND eight a.m. My head was pounding. I felt like I was having heart palpitations. My mind began racing again about my breast cancer diagnosis from the day before. Tears rolled down my face. "Lord, what am I going to do?" I got out of bed and began pacing around the house. I tried to find something to do to take my mind off it. I decided to call my parents. I just wanted to hear their voices, which soothed my spirit. They both answered the phone. I wished them a Happy New Year and they did the same.

"So, what do you have planned for today?" they asked me.

"Nothing. Just resting," I replied with tears in my eyes. I tried to keep my voice calm and cheery, but that proved difficult to do. It was breaking my heart that I had this bad news. I couldn't bring myself to tell them, especially not on New Year's Day. I did not want to ruin their holiday. My family had been through enough tragedy and bad news around the holidays, and I didn't want to be a contributing factor to that. After I got off of the phone with them,

I began taking down my Christmas decorations. I removed the garland from around the fireplace, then began working on taking down the Christmas tree. I got halfway done with taking down the Christmas tree, then sat in the middle of the floor next to the tree and cried and screamed uncontrollably. I was thinking, "Lord, I know this is a journey you need me to complete for the greater good of helping people, but this is so hard to even consider right now!"

After a while, I reached for the phone and decided I had to call someone. I needed to tell my friend who was also a breast cancer survivor. I knew she would understand. I called her and her phone went to voice mail. I left her a message and said, "Call me as soon as you can." It was still early, and she was not a morning person, so I knew she was probably still asleep.

I called my oldest sister. I told her everything. Even though I knew she could be very emotional about things and didn't know how she would handle my news, I had to call her. She answered the phone and said, "Happy New Year, sis! I saw the pictures you posted from the event you went to last night. You looked absolutely stunning! I loved the outfit! Tell me more about it!"

I told her a little about the event, then I said, "Sis, I have something to tell you."

"Sis, what's wrong?" she said. The tone in her voice changed.

There was no easy way for me to tell her, so I ripped the bandage right off.

"I have breast cancer." As the words came out of my mouth, I began to cry again. She became very quiet, took some deep breaths, and with the sound of tears in her voice she said, "Sis, everything is going to be okay. We will get through this." She asked if I had told anyone else and I told her that I had tried to call my friend and did not get an answer. She said, "Are you going to be okay? Do you need me?"

"No, I am not okay, and I do need you," I said.

"Okay. Let me pack my bag and I am on my way."

She lived two-and-a-half hours from me yet dropped everything to come and rush to be at my side. I felt somewhat relieved that I told somebody, yet my heart was still aching.

I managed to finish taking the Christmas decorations down, packed them in boxes, and stored them back in the closet. By that time, my girlfriend returned my call.

"Is everything okay?" she asked.

I said, "No, can you come over?"

She lived twenty-five to thirty minutes from me and said, "Okay, I am on my way."

I showered and waited on my couch for her to arrive. She rang the doorbell and I let her in. She looked concerned. I invited her to come in and sit on the couch. Once again, there was no easy way for me to tell her, so I had to rip the bandage off a second time. I started by saying, "I did not want to tell you this last night because I did not want to ruin the evening, but I did get my biopsy results back and I have breast cancer."

She hugged me and said, "Oh, Crystal, I am so sorry."

I laid my head in her lap and cried like a baby. She rubbed my arm and shoulders and provided words of comfort. I remember she tried to make me feel better by saying, "God is just giving you some baby cancer, just enough for you to have the experience yet be able to help other cancer patients even more." I knew she was right, but nothing anybody could say offered me comfort. The tears dried up briefly. After about an hour of my friend at my side, my sister arrived. When I opened the door, I hugged her, and the tears began to flow again. My sister and my friend both continued to offer me support. They both kept saying that God had been preparing me all this time to go through this breast cancer journey. The lymphedema certification, serving on the cancer committee, specializing in cancer rehabilitation, starting a nonprofit, in which all of the board members were breast cancer survivors except me. They were right. I was being prepared all this time and did not even know it. We continued to talk. We ordered food: lemon pepper wings and french fries, to be exact. I needed comfort food. Well, there went my detox for the year! We sat around the table and talked and joked. I was able to laugh and get in a smile or two. My friend left that night, and my sister and I were alone together.

January 2, 2020—upon waking the next morning, I was still

very tearful. My mind began reeling again trying to process everything that was happening. I made my way downstairs. My sister was still asleep on the couch. She heard me come downstairs and woke up and said, "Are you okay?"

"No," I answered. I sat down next to her, laid my head on her shoulder, and began to cry again.

She also shed tears but reassuringly said, "Sis, it's going to be okay. I promise. We will get through this together."

I kept telling her how much I did not want to tell my other sister and my parents. We had enough tragedy in our family around the holidays and I did not want to add to it.

She said, "This is your story to tell. You tell whoever you want to whenever you are ready. I won't say anything to anybody."

I could always tell my sister anything and she always came through on her promises.

After I finished having another good cry, my sister and I continued to talk about my diagnosis. I mentioned how my OBGYN gave me a recommendation for a breast surgeon, but after looking up the practice online, it did not resonate with my spirit. I was becoming stressed about having to make a decision about the doctors I wanted to use for my care. Although I previously worked for a large health system in Georgia, I was familiar with some of the doctors and personally did not want to use them for my care based on my professional knowledge and experience at the type of work they performed for breast cancer patients. I was becoming overwhelmed as I searched for breast surgeons and read reviews online. I said to my sister, "I need to ask my plastic surgery friend and soror who she would recommend as a breast surgeon, but I'm going to tell her my patients want a good recommendation because I don't want anybody to know about my diagnosis yet."

I met this plastic surgeon at a Paint Gwinnett Pink event for breast cancer awareness that was held in October 2019. It was the same event that I ran into the massage therapist again that I was renting my office space from. I carried folders of my information around, and I went to her table to introduce myself. She was a new plastic surgeon in the area. Ironically, she also specialized in microsurgery for lymphedema. What were the odds! We connected and eventually went out for dinner together to catch up. I found out that she had also taken a leap of faith by leaving her position as a physician/surgeon at a prominent medical center to start her own practice in Duluth, Georgia. As we continued to talk, I quickly learned that our journeys starting our businesses were parallel. We both expressed how we had experienced systemic racism and how we had to work and fight harder as Black women to prove ourselves and to be heard in our professions, even though we were smart and highly educated. A bonus was that we were also sorority sisters of Alpha Kappa Alpha Sorority, Inc. I definitely respected her hustle.

Literally within an hour, my phone rang. The display showed the plastic surgeon's name. My sister and I both looked at each other wide-eyed in disbelief. I answered the phone. She was calling to wish me a Happy New Year. She also thanked me for taking care of her patients that she had referred to me for their postoperative care. I took the opportunity to ask her to recommend a good breast surgeon. She, without hesitation, gave me a recommendation. Then she said, "I have her information right here. Would you like me to give you the number?"

"Sure!" I replied. I thanked her for the patient referrals as well as the breast surgeon referral. After the phone call, my sister and I said, "Wow!"

"Sis, I am scared of you," she said. "You literally just said you need a recommendation for a breast surgeon, and she calls your phone. What are the odds of that!"

"I know, sis, I know!" I said.

Our minds were literally blown away.

Later that day, my friend sent my sister and me a text message about free tickets to a comedy show later in the evening. I looked at my sister and said, "I could use some laughter. Let's go!" We met her at the comedy club that night, and I must say I had a wonderful time. I needed the laughter. Comedian Shuler King was the headliner, and he was absolutely hilarious! Even with a breast cancer diagnosis looming over my head, that night I chose joy and laughter over doom, gloom, and depression.

## 16

## First Quarter 2020— Consciousness and Confirmation

THE YEAR 2020 CONTINUED TO COME IN LIKE A roaring lion. I was still trying to process being diagnosed with breast cancer and the impacts it would have on the rest of my life. I had so many things to do and so many decisions to make. I was scheduled for a second biopsy on January 6 to sample the second cluster of cancer cells in my left breast. This time it wasn't so bad because I knew what to expect. Still, the drilling sound of the biopsy needle and the pressure and the act of being in that mammogram machine was horrible and something I hoped I never had to experience again. After the biopsy, I had a candid conversation with the radiologist.

I asked, "Who do you recommend as a breast surgeon?"

She said what I knew she would say, which was the breast surgeon who I worked in the same hospital system with.

I said, "I don't care about convenience or proximity to me. If you were in my shoes, who would you go and see?"

She gave me the names of two surgeons. I stored the info in my head. I still ventured to that appointment alone and went to work as usual afterward. Working was my safety net and allowed me to take my mind off of my situation and continue to be a help and blessing to others.

On January 7, I had a breast MRI with and without contrast. I was fine until I sat in the lobby and began to look at the paperwork I had to fill out. Some of the questions were:

Do you have cancer? If so what kind?

Have you had any cancer treatment? If so, please provide the dates.

Filling out this paperwork and the questions asking if I had cancer triggered me emotionally. I tried to remain calm as I ventured to this appointment solo yet again.

The MRI tech came to the waiting room to get me. I was taken to the patient changing area where I put on a gown, then escorted to a chair to wait to be taken to the MRI machine. I was becoming more emotional by the minute. Tears began welling up in my eyes, but I tried my best to blink them away. The tech entered the room and said very nonchalantly, "So you have breast cancer." As I said yes, the tears began to roll down my cheeks. I could no longer contain them. I was thinking, "To this tech, I'm just another number and another patient she has to treat and she acts as if my diagnosis doesn't even matter." I took several deep breaths and proceeded back to the breast MRI machine. I had to lie on my stomach with my large pendulous breasts hanging down in the machine. Because of my large breasts, the tech and assistant had to reposition me several times because my breasts were literally hanging down to the bottom of the platform.

The tech said to me, "Is your left breast bigger than your right?"

At that moment, something in me snapped. I let her have it!

"Of course, it is bigger!" I said. "This is the side where the cancer is, and I just had two biopsies so of course it is bigger and swollen!"

Her eyes got big, and she swallowed hard and mustered to say, "Okay."

All sorts of emotions went through my mind. I was furious at this point. Furious, scared, nervous, anxious, hurt, saddened, overwhelmed all at the same time. Here I was having another test to determine if there were any other areas of cancer in my breasts or in my lymph nodes. Luckily, after it was all said and done, the imaging showed the same areas of concern in my breast as the biopsy and mammogram and showed no evidence of cancer in the lymph nodes or right breast. The pathology report said that my cancer was 99 percent estrogen positive and progesterone negative. Honestly, I was hoping that all of these tests would show that there was indeed no cancer anywhere at all. However, there was no way for me to escape having to deal with it.

Now that I had further testing done and everything was confirmed, it was now time for me to tell my parents and my other sister. I wanted to be sure about the testing and diagnosis before I told anyone else. I absolutely dreaded having to make the call, but it had to be done. Here I went again, having to rip the bandage off. I first called my middle sister and told her I was going to conference Mom and Dad in on the call. She was concerned, but said, "Okay." Once everybody was on the phone, I took a deep breath.

"There is no easy way for me to say this," I said. "But I got the results back from my breast biopsy and I have breast cancer."

"Oh no!" I heard my sister say.

I proceeded to tell them that I had another biopsy and breast MRI which all confirmed the diagnosis. My parents were quiet, in shock.

My dad started crying and said, "Baby, I know God's got this. His hands are all over it. He showed it to me, and I've already seen it."

I can count the number of times on one hand that I have seen or heard my dad cry. It tore my heart into a million pieces to hear him cry and break down. My mom was a tough cookie, and she did not cry on the phone. With shakiness in her voice, she said, "Just know that whatever you need us to do we are here, and we are praying for you."

I broke down and cried again.

"I'm so sorry," I repeated over and over and over again. I kept apologizing to them for having to break their hearts with this news. My parents were angels on earth. Now they had to see their baby girl go through this. They were very concerned about me being at home by myself, but I told them how my oldest sister, came up to be with me and that I had my friend to support me in their absence. I told them that I did not yet know my next steps, but I was in the process of finding a breast surgeon and plastic surgeon to meet with to get this cancer out of my body.

That same week, an oncologist referred a patient to me for breast cancer rehab. Her office called me to schedule the patient, who was at the office at the time. I was on another call and told the front office coordinator to send over the patient's info and phone number and I would return the call for scheduling as soon as possible. This was my friend's medical oncologist when she went through her breast cancer journey. The doctor also held cancer support groups at her medical practice. My nonprofit organization Champions Can! had a Survivorship Day Party event in September 2019. My friend had asked the oncologist to speak at the event about the importance of cancer screening and detection. She agreed. At the event we became more acquainted, and I graciously thanked her for her time and impact at the event.

As I read the patient information that was sent over to me, I sat there with my mouth and eyes wide open. She was being referred to me to restore ROM and for breast cancer rehab. According to the medical records, this patient was forty-seven years old and had the same breast cancer diagnosis as I did (DCIS). She underwent a double mastectomy with DIEP flap reconstruction and was currently on hormone therapy. She did not have chemotherapy or radiation. As I kept reading her record, I was in disbelief. The same breast surgeon my plastic surgeon friend recommended to me was the same breast surgeon this patient had. I did not recognize the name of the plastic surgeon that she used, but I felt that God was again confirming the doctors that I should use for my journey and was laying things out in front of me. My heart began beating extremely fast.

I reached out to the patient to schedule her for an appointment with Eminence Physical Therapy. I asked her numerous questions about her diagnosis, so I would know how to best treat her with physical therapy and to help decide about my diagnosis and course of action. She was telling me about her family history of breast cancer and that she decided to have a double mastectomy. She became emotional and tearful about the recent death of her ex-husband and potentially losing her home as she continued to be out of work and support her three children. She also shared with me about losing some friends along the way when she told them about her breast cancer diagnosis. I asked her, "Physical therapy aside, what do you need? How else can I help you?"

Behind a shaky voice, she said, "I don't know what I need. Nobody ever asks me what it is that I need."

"No pressure," I said. "Think about it and if I can support you in any way, I am here." I told her about the book I had written for my nonprofit organization, *The Elements of Cancer Survivorship: A Guide to Navigating the Journey*. I got her address and said, "I want to send you something in the mail." She expressed many thanks.

Something deep in my spirit told me to share with this patient my recent diagnosis. Once I told her, her emotions shifted positively and she said, "Oh my God, Dr. Champion, how can I help you?" The tables had turned from me encouraging her to her pouring it back into me. She shared with me how she had been taking holy communion every day for healing since her diagnosis and how much it was making a difference in her life. She said, "This whole experience has shown me that I am not yet walking in my purpose. There is something more that I am supposed to be doing but I just don't know what it is yet." We continued to talk and minister to each other as she also talked about the wonderful experiences she had with her healthcare providers to include the breast surgeon, plastic surgeon, and medical oncologist. One hour later, we said our goodbyes and vowed to keep in touch with each other.

"Lord, thank you!" I was so ecstatic that God had shown me clearly who I needed to be a part of my medical team. I called to make an appointment with the breast surgeon and, to my surprise, got an appointment very quickly. To prepare for the appointment, I needed to have all of my medical records and previous testing results. I called the nurse navigator at the breast center, and she said, "We can have your records and MRI CD ready for you to pick up by five p.m. today." I ventured to the hospital to pick up my medical information. I was in deep thought as I headed back home. As I continued to think about what I need to do next, I turned onto my street. I went around the deep curve and spotted a black van in front of me. It had a logo on the back of it in writing that read, "God Is Dope." Hmmm. I felt that it was yet another sign. "Yes, God, you are DOPE, even though this is difficult." It was further reassurance and confirmation to me that I was going to be just fine after all and that I had nothing to worry about.

On January 10, I had my first appointment with the breast surgical oncologist. Before the appointment, for some reason, my dad kept telling me to see another doctor and get a second opinion on the pathology report. I considered it and decided to act on his advice. I had my slides sent from one hospital to the new hospital where I would be receiving my care and had to wait a few days for the results. My friend accompanied me to the appointment. The breast surgeon's demeanor was very calming, and I felt an immediate sense of ease when she entered the room. I had sent her office my medical records ahead of time for her review. She told me that she had gotten the pathology report back from the second opinion I requested and that the report was consistent with my initial diagnosis of DCIS of the left breast. She pulled out a dry erase marker and began to draw on her whiteboard details about my diagnosis, what it meant, and how it was treated. She told me I did not require chemotherapy, but I would need surgery, possibly radiation, and would need to be on hormone therapy for five years in addition to being monitored by her every six months for the next two to three years. She kindly asked me, "So what are you thinking you want to do?"

"Chop them both off and let me do DIEP flap reconstruction. I don't want to have to do this again and I don't want radiation."

"You really want a double mastectomy?" she said.

"Yes!" I said enthusiastically.

She told me that based on the cancer being in two different quadrants of my breast, the recommended treatment would be a mastectomy. A lumpectomy would not be an option. She also said that even though my testing showed that there was no cancer in my lymph nodes, she still wanted to do a lymph node biopsy just to be sure that there was no incidence of micro invasion. I dropped my head in my hands. I already knew that having lymph nodes removed meant that I was at risk for getting lymphedema, the very same condition I treat my patients for day in and day out. *Whew, Lord! This is a lot!* I thought.

I asked her who she recommended for a plastic surgeon. She gave me the name of a colleague. I asked if she had ever worked with my plastic surgeon friend, and she said she hadn't but was willing to work with her for my sake. In the same breath, she said that she had a great working relationship with the plastic surgeon that she had just mentioned and highly recommended him. My mind was put at ease as she confirmed what I already wanted to do. I left the appointment feeling much better about the situation. Her office arranged for me to see the recommended plastic surgeon. Of course, I did my research on him online and looked at post-surgical results on his website. It looked like he did amazing work!

On January 22, I met with the plastic surgeon. My middle sister accompanied me to the appointment. I had learned my lesson about going to appointments alone! The plastic surgeon was young and had a very pleasant demeanor. He reviewed my file and, like the breast surgeon, he asked me what I wanted to do. I told him I wanted to proceed with a double mastectomy with a DIEP flap reconstruction. He also presented me with the option for tissue expanders with implant reconstruction. I knew I did not want anything foreign in my body, so I wanted my reconstruction to be as natural as possible. He really was patient and took his time with answering my questions as well as explaining to me both pros and cons of each procedure, including a three-day ICU stay and the possibility of tissue flap death with the DIEP flap reconstruction. One of my biggest concerns was recovery time. Financially, being self-employed and the only person running my business, that meant that *everything* had to come to a stop, and my income would not be flowing during my recovery. A lot of people don't realize that being self-employed means giving up the luxury of having benefits such as paid time off and extended illness bank that you can pull from. Even though I had my own practice, I also did contract work for a medical device company. This surgery meant that I would have to stop both jobs because both were physically demanding. It was concerning. However, I had to get my health in check and get rid of this cancer to even continue working. He did tell me that because my breasts were so large that I had a lot of extra tissue to be managed which could yield a poor cosmetic outcome. I would also lose both nipples and was not a candidate for a nipple-sparing mastectomy, especially being that one cluster of cells was two centimeters behind my left nipple. He drew a picture of the incisions that I would have.

"Your breasts are so large," he said, "and it looks like you should have had a breast reduction a long time ago, but being that we want to do surgery and for safety, we will have to manage it all with one surgery."

My middle sister had a breast reduction surgery with the same scars that I was going to have and kept reassuring me that her recovery was easy and I would be fine.

With all of the information provided to me, I opted to pursue the double mastectomy with DIEP flap reconstruction. I was told that his office coordinator would check my insurance benefits for authorization for the procedure. He also asked me when I potentially wanted to have surgery and I said ASAP, definitely before the end of February. I calculated that it would give me enough time to finish up some of my therapy clients and get things in order to take a break from my business.

The surgery coordinator checked the schedule and the earliest date of which both he and the breast surgeon were available was February 18. This was perfect because my oldest sister was out of school for a break and would be able to bring my parents up for the surgery day. Again, I left the appointment still concerned about what I was about to endure but at ease. I was so thankful that both doctors made me feel comfortable. Their demeanors were settling to my spirit. I did not feel the need to seek a second opinion. Besides, God literally put those physicians in my path, and I was learning to trust God even more than ever before.

Later that evening, I was scheduled to speak at a cancer support group at an oncology office about cancer rehab and lymphedema. Even though my head was about to explode with what I was dealing with, I found comfort in continuing to educate others. My friend also attended the support group and said, "You are the strongest person I know. You just got diagnosed with breast cancer, yet you still were so inspiring and gave hope and knowledge to everybody in that room." To make things even better, I found out that one of the women in the support group also had the same breast surgeon I had just selected and raved about the excellent care she received from her. Wow, God, you did it again. I was receiving ongoing confirmation that I was on the right track concerning my medical care.

Two days later, I received a call from the plastic surgeon's office asking me if I would be able to speak via phone to the doctor around seven p.m. that evening about the upcoming surgery. I agreed and the doctor called me from his personal cell phone as promised. He delivered some news that once again caused my heart to sink into the pits of my stomach. I had a short-term medical insurance plan. He told me that my insurance company would not authorize the DIEP flap reconstruction and stated that would make determination of claim payment once all of my medical records were sent in after surgery. In other words, he said that it was too great of a risk for his practice to potentially forego payment for this surgery, but he was willing to operate on my case free of charge and not bill the insurance company. I was very grateful to him for that, however, I had a thousand questions. My legs were shaking uncontrollably. I asked him what my other options were. He told me that he had already spoken with the breast surgeon, and they agreed that it would be okay to proceed with a lumpectomy with sentinel lymph node biopsy (SLNB) along with a breast reduction of the right breast to match. He stated that the breast surgeon was okay with the procedure because I had very large breasts and was confident that enough breast tissue could be safely removed without me being severely disfigured or requiring any other type of reconstruction. Shoot! A lumpectomy meant that I would have to be subjected to radiation, which was one of the reasons I wanted to have a double mastectomy. I was even more on edge, but the decision was completely out of my control. The plastic surgeon graciously said he had research articles about oncoplastic breast reductions in the setting of cancer prior to double mastectomy were safely done for women with large breasts for overall better cosmetic outcomes. He was very reassuring and said, "Crystal, honestly this is a blessing in disguise. If down the road you want to proceed with a double mastectomy once you get an insurance that will authorize the procedure, you will be in a much better situation to preserve your natural nipples as well as you will have a better cosmetic outcome because all the extra tissue will be managed with a lesser chance for incisional problems and tissue death. We really couldn't ask for a better situation in your case right now."

As confident as he was, my mind began racing all over again about my course of treatment and the diagnosis. As promised, he emailed me two research articles about women in my situation. It looked very promising. However, I was so unsure. Nothing seemed to be happening the way I had anticipated. Even though friends and family tried to console me and reassure me that the whole thing was God's way of stopping me from having a surgery that was so drastic and a recovery that would have been much more difficult, I still did not have peace or comfort about the situation. It was completely out of my control. I had no choice but to trust God on this one. So far, He has been confirming things for me, so I had to keep trusting and believing. I kept hearing my dad's words in my head: "God's got this."

One night, I had a very vivid dream. I was on the back of a pickup truck, alone. I could not see who was driving the truck.

The weather outside was very stormy. The rain was torrential and trees around me were violently swaying in the wind, some snapping and falling to the ground. I was exposed to all of the elements. The only thing I had to protect me was a thin quilt that I pulled over my head and body for the duration of the storm. After a while, the truck stopped, and the storm stopped. I emerged from underneath the quilt. Everything around me was damaged or destroyed, yet I was untouched. When I woke up, I was amazed. I lay in bed trying to decipher the dream. I couldn't see the driver but had to trust the driver to get me out of the storm. It appeared symbolic of having to trust God to get me through this cancer diagnosis. The thin quilt was symbolic of divine protection. The storm was symbolic of a rough time up ahead, but the fact that I was unharmed in the process told me that God would protect me and guide me through. That dream confirmed for me that everything was going to be more than okay, I just had to trust and believe and continue to let God be my driver.

I received a phone call from my friend and nonprofit secretary that our VP had been taken to the hospital again. She had fallen at home and had a seizure. I went to the hospital to visit her. Her husband was present in the room, but my VP was sleeping from medications. She was having seizures, and, unfortunately, the tumors in her brain began to grow again. She lost function in her right arm and was having difficulty walking. I remember her face and skin glowing. She looked flawless even though she had monitors hooked up to her head measuring brain activity. I held her and her husband's hand and prayed over her. She woke up briefly. I could tell that she was trying to figure out who I was, and I had to remind her. After a while, she kept saying, "So how are you?" She asked me multiple times as if she could sense something was wrong with me. I tried to maintain my composure. I managed to smile and say, "All is well with me. Don't worry about me. I am more concerned about you." I blinked back my tears as I did not have the heart to tell her that I had just been diagnosed with breast cancer, the very same beast that she was in the fight for her life with. I kissed her on the cheek and bid her goodbye. After leaving her, I sat in my car in the parking garage and cried. I was overwhelmed with emotion. Here my VP was, who has been fighting metastatic breast cancer since I first met her, and she was still fighting for her life. And now here I was, about to start my own fight against breast cancer. It was all so unfair! I had to dry up my tears and shift my mindset. My VP was giving me strength. She was determined and always talked about how God was her healer. This time, the doctors felt the need to operate. She had a craniotomy to remove the tumors and after a few weeks, was transferred to a rehabilitation center to recover. She still did not know about my diagnosis.

On January 26, as I was researching things on the internet about my diagnosis, I turned on the news. Breaking news flashed on the screen. Basketball-great Kobe Bryant was killed at the age of forty-one, along with his thirteen-year-old daughter, in a horrific helicopter crash. I was stunned and shocked! The news completely took my mind off of the difficult encounter I was about to have with upcoming breast cancer treatment. I thought to myself, "Lord, just when you think you are going through a rough time, someone else is going through something one thousand times worse." I couldn't help but think about Kobe's wife, Vanessa Bryant, and their other two children. A wife had lost her spouse/soulmate and her child. The children lost a dad and their sister. That is an unimaginable amount of grief for one person to endure. My mindset about my current situation shifted. I knew that as painful as it was, I had to be grateful for my situation. I did not have to have chemotherapy and lose my hair. The cancer was localized and had not spread. I had the chance to have surgery and try to get back to a life of normalcy. I still had a life to live and continued purpose to fulfill. Unlike Kobe Bryant, his life ended, and he was no longer alive to finish living out whatever other dreams and purposeful things he had planned. Life is fleeting and short. One incident could change the course of your life forever. In the setting of death and grief over Kobe Bryant—a prominent figure in the Black community—I was still grateful that once my battle with breast cancer was over, I would still have the opportunity to use the experience to better the lives of the patients I serve through my business and nonprofit.

## 17

## Showtime or No Time

MY SURGERY DATE WAS QUICKLY APPROACHING. I still had lots of things to prepare before surgery so that I wouldn't be stressed during my recovery. I had to wrap up things with my foundation as well as my practice and contract work. I had to file both my business and personal tax returns because I knew that my recovery would put me close to the tax deadline. I wanted to lessen the load of having to deal with anything other than recovering from surgery so I could get back to work. The hospital where I had surgery called me and told me that since my astronomical $10,000 deductible had not been met, I had to pay the remaining deductible before having surgery. It caught me off guard because surely, I thought, with all of the imaging and testing I had done, the deductible should have been met. The hospital verified my insurance, and I also checked the insurance website to find out that once I reached the initial $5,000, the rest of the claims went under a medical review. Needless to say, I had to pay over $4,000 to meet the rest of the deductible. Whatever. It had to be done. Initially, I was planning to stay at my middle sister's house after surgery. Then I realized that I would have a much better recovery at my own home and in my own bed. I made arrangements for my mom to stay with me to help me after surgery. She told me that she would stay with me as long as I needed her to.

February 14 was my last scheduled day of work before surgery. I had clients that morning, then had a hair appointment scheduled with my middle sister later that afternoon. I woke up with a nagging dry cough. I felt fine, so I didn't really think anything of it. I went about my day as usual. Once I got to my sister's salon, I continued coughing. She said, "You sure are coughing a lot. Are you feeling okay?"

"I feel fine," I said, "but I will be glad when I can get back home and take something to try to get rid of this cough."

The next evening, I was scheduled to go to an SWV concert at the Fox Theater with my friend. She had won tickets on the radio, and I certainly wanted to go and enjoy myself and take my mind off of my upcoming surgery. My nagging cough was getting progressively worse, and I was feeling not so great, but I refused to miss the concert. I got dressed, went to the concert as planned, had a great time, and headed back home. Once I got ready for bed, I noticed I was feeling a little worse. I just wanted to go to sleep.

The next day, Sunday morning, February 16, I started to feel even worse. I woke up with a fever of 100.1, body aches, severe teeth-chattering chills, loss of appetite, and a relentless cough. I was so fatigued that all I wanted to do was sleep and lie down. I was scheduled to go to the surgery center on Monday, February 17, to have the mapping of my lymph nodes done in preparation for surgery. My surgery was scheduled so early on the eighteenth that it would not allow time for the lymph node mapping to be completed. I was on the couch all day, feeling horrible. I did not want to take a lot of medication because I did not want anything to interfere with the anesthesia that I would have to have for surgery. I rarely got sick beyond a seasonal cold or sinus infection. I had never felt this bad. I literally kept saying to myself, "I really don't feel good."

The seventeenth arrived, and I was scheduled to go to the surgery center. I still felt like crap, but I had to keep pressing forward. My parents and my oldest sister arrived at my house in time to accompany me to the appointment as well as to see where I would have to go for surgery. I was anxious. My parents and sister waited for me in the waiting room. They showed looks of concern as the technician called me back to prepare me for the lymph node mapping. I lay on the table, and the attending radiologist for the day injected my left breast with a contrast dye to be used for the lymph node mapping. Here I was again having my left breast poked and prodded on. I was so over it! After about thirty minutes, I was taken to the other side of the hospital to an imaging machine to have the pictures taken of the lymph nodes. The technician drew the location of the lymph nodes to be taken on my skin with a surgical marker. After the procedure, I was escorted back to the waiting room with my family, and we left. We were hungry, so we stopped at a seafood restaurant to have dinner. I was still sick, coughing uncontrollably but tried to suppress it long enough to be in public and have dinner. I was very anxious and ready to get the surgery over with. I had to be at the surgery center at six a.m. to get prepped, even though my surgery was not until ten a.m. that morning. I wanted to get to bed early in order to have a good night's sleep. After getting back home from dinner, I was feeling bad again. I was drinking hot lemon and honey tea, had cough drops, yet nothing was helping my cough. I was panicking because I still had a low-grade temp of 99.0. "They are going to cancel my surgery," I thought. I frantically began searching the internet for indications for surgery cancellation. Everything I saw kept saying to notify your medical provider. However, I had cancer that I needed to get out of my body, and I wasn't going to let anything stop me! My sister was concerned and kept helping monitor my temperature. Needless to say, that night I was up coughing all night and did not get any sleep AT ALL. I was exhausted, felt horrible, yet I had to get up, shower with my antibacterial scrub, and head to the surgery center. Me, my parents, and sister held hands, stood in a circle in the living room, and prayed before we left my house. Afterward, we all piled into my sister's SUV. I was sure to pack a pillow for the ride home and wear comfortable clothing to put on again after surgery.

My surgery was a day procedure, and I was expected to be released to go home that same day. The ride was quiet. It was dark outside. I kept my eyes closed and prayed the entire time.

We arrived at the surgery center a bit early. I made sure to use the bathroom. My nerves were on level twenty. My sister and dad were quiet, however my mom was nervous and was talking her way through everything. She was making me more anxious. I just wanted peace and quiet and time to meditate before the procedure. I checked-in to the registration area and was escorted to the surgery waiting area. The receptionist had me fill out paperwork and explained to me and my family how the process was going to work from start of surgery to post-op recovery waiting. About thirty minutes later, a nurse came to get me from the waiting room to get started. I took a deep breath, looked back at my family, and waved before disappearing through the double doors.

The nurse put me in a pre-op waiting area and had me change into a gown and socks. She took my personal belongings. Afterward, she took my vitals. I told her that I did not feel well and that I had a dry, non-productive cough and a fever. She listened to my lungs with the stethoscope and said that everything sounded clear. She took my temperature orally, which was also normal. My oxygen saturation level was normal, but my blood pressure was slightly elevated because I was very nervous. Shortly after, the anesthesiologist on my case entered my room to go over some details with me. I told her that I was not feeling well.

"Unless you are deathly ill with a high fever, we are still going to proceed with your surgery," she said.

I breathed a sigh of relief. My sister was allowed to come back and sit with me. She joked around, trying to calm me down. The breast surgeon also stopped by to go over logistics and made me laugh with her great sense of humor. She gave my sister and I recommendations for movies and TV shows to watch to make me laugh once I got home to recover. The plastic surgeon also stopped by to make final surgical markings on both breasts where the incisions would be made.

Before I could proceed with surgery, I had to have wires placed in the left breast. I was having a wire-guided biopsy. The wires were placed to bracket off the area of cancer that had to be removed so the surgeon could be sure she removed it all. Let me tell you, the wire placement was the most traumatizing part of my surgery. It brought back memories of my mammograms and biopsies that led to my breast cancer diagnosis. I was placed in the mammography machine so that the radiologist and mammography tech could see where to place the wires. My breast was injected with a local anesthetic. After what felt like hours of my left breast being poked and smashed, I was a complete wreck. The radiologist kept taking pictures after the wires were placed. I sat in the chair, in tears, and in pain, even though I had pain meds. She came back into the room and told me she needed to insert an additional set of wires because, upon reviewing the films, she saw more cancer. Oh my God! I had to step back into the machine and get poked with more wires. I was put in a wheelchair and taken back to the pre-op waiting room. I saw both of my doctors standing in the hallway.

"There she is!" they said.

Because of the additional wire placement, my surgery was delayed by at least an hour. I had six wires poking out of the side of my left breast. Once I sat back in my chair, I was in tears. The nurse would only allow a few family members back at a time to see me. My mom and oldest sister came back first. They were smiling until they saw my eyes welled up with tears and the tear stains on my cheeks.

"What's wrong?" they asked me.

I opened my gown and showed them the wires and told them how painful it was and how I felt traumatized being in that machine all over again.

Shortly after, two OR nurses came to get me for surgery. As I was wheeled into the room, my breast surgeon was standing next to the operating table and introduced me to the team. I was helped up onto the table. The surgeon held my hand and rubbed my arm and said, "You will be fine. It's go time!" The oxygen mask was put over my face. I kept saying to myself, "Jesus, Jesus, Jesus." I was asked to take a few deep breaths, then I went to sleep.

I woke up in the post-op recovery room. I remember looking to my left and seeing the nurse sitting next to me looking at the monitor. I was still hooked to an IV and had a nasal cannula. I was in a reclined position, but I felt like I needed to sit up. I kept trying to wiggle around.

"I need to sit up!" I yelled.

The nurse told me to calm down so I wouldn't pull out my IV. She adjusted the bed for me to make me more comfortable. Once I realized where I was, the medical professional in me came out. I managed to look over at the monitor and saw that all of my vital signs were stable. My hospital training and ability to read monitors surely came in handy! I was so groggy. I was able to look down the front of my gown enough to see that I had on a compression bra and lots of bandages and padding. I could not see my breasts. All I knew was I was in pain. My oldest sister entered shortly after.

"Did they save my nipples?" I asked first.

She smiled and said, "Yes, sis, you still have your nipples."

She tried to tell me that the breast surgeon came into the waiting area and updated my family after everything was done and said that the surgery went well, and I would have the final pathology results by the time of my next post-op follow-up appointment already scheduled for a week later. Before I could blink my eyes, my shirt, shoes, and pants were on, and I was whisked out of the room in a wheelchair. I was escorted into the lobby with the rest of my family, including my parents, middle sister, brother-in-law, and niece and nephew. My oldest sister pulled the car around to the veranda.

The nurse tech escorted me outside. I was groggy and everything was a blur. I remember the nurse tech yelling at a car behind my sister to move out of the way so that I could be assisted into the car. She helped me into the front seat, placed a pillow across my chest, adjusted my seatbelt, and off we went. I slept the entire way home and don't remember much of the ride.

My sister helped me out of the car when I got home. I was hungry and attempted to sit at the table to eat some chicken noodle soup while taking some pain medication. I ate half the bowl of soup. I was so exhausted and all I wanted to do was sleep. My sister and mom helped me upstairs and helped me change into pajamas. I had great difficulty trying to lean over or lift both arms, and my left arm and chest were completely numb. Again, I looked down at my chest at the bra and bandages but did not want to see what was underneath. I got into bed, propped up with a bunch of pillows, and drifted off to sleep.

I woke up at three a.m., tears rolling down my face. I was in pain. My pain medication had worn off. I yelled out for my sister. I was trying to get myself out of bed but was in too much pain to move. She brought me a bottle of water, ice packs, and made sure I took my pain medicine. We set a timer on my phone so I would be sure not to miss my next dose.

My sister had to leave the next day. My dad was going to go back home so he could keep an eye on the house and my mom was going to stay with me to take care of me. While my mom cooked breakfast, my sister helped me with a sponge bath. I was still in so much pain. The numbness in my chest and arm felt like a thousand bumblebees had landed on me. I was so ashamed that I could not even use my hands to help wash my body and put lotion on. My sister had to literally wash my ass. I was not used to having to be helped. This was the worst. She helped me remove my compression bra because I wanted to see what my new breasts looked like. I hated seeing the anchor scars I had, but I must admit, they were perky and lifted even though I was still very swollen. After my humiliating sponge bath, we ventured downstairs to have breakfast. As my dad and sister left, my dad kept looking back at me through the door as if he didn't want to leave and was majorly concerned.

Me and my mom were left alone. I went back upstairs, made sure I was on schedule with my pain meds, had my ice packs, and slept the day away. My mom made some homemade vegetable soup for dinner. I managed to make it downstairs to eat a few spoonfuls, then back to my room to sleep.

That night, I woke up again in pain. Apparently, I forgot to set my timer to stay on schedule with my pain meds. I struggled to get out of bed and made my way downstairs. My mom was still up, sitting on the couch watching TV. I walked slowly in pain and sat down next to her. She got my ice packs and pain meds. She teared up seeing me crying in pain. I am very strong. I rarely cried or let my family see me cry. At this point, I was hurting so bad I couldn't help it. She didn't have words to say, but rubbed my arm and hand and said, "It is going to be okay."

*18*

## The Shake-Up and the Wake-Up

APPROXIMATELY TWO DAYS AFTER SURGERY, I WAS getting calls from the business office of the hospital where I had all of my biopsies, mammograms, and MRIs. I had a balance due because I had to meet my astronomical deductible of $10,000. Five thousand of it had been met at that particular facility. I was told what my balance was, and was asked if I wanted to make a payment that day using a credit or debit card. *Really?* I thought to myself. Here I was in pain, lying in bed, trying to recover from surgery, and they were already calling me asking for money! My head was spinning because I wasn't working and trying not to blow through my savings. I made a payment, then asked if I could be placed on a payment plan. The rep told me I could. I also asked if I could apply for financial assistance. She said she would email the application. I figured it was worth a try to ease some of the burden. After all, I had bills to pay. I was single and did not have a spouse or any other additional income. I was on my own and needed to stay afloat until I could get back to work.

I could feel myself sinking into a depression. Even though my mom was at home helping to take care of me, she barely saw me. I would come out of my room long enough to eat, then go right back upstairs, watch TV, and sleep. I binged several TV shows, but one of them I wish I hadn't watched. It was a reality-dating show about finding love. It made me think about the fact that I was single and didn't have my "ride or die" life partner to go through this journey with me. Of course, I had the support of my close friend and my family, but it was not the same as having a spouse or life partner to lean on. Just before being diagnosed, I was dating a very successful stockbroker.

I trusted him enough to tell him about my diagnosis because I knew he was a prayer warrior and a strong person of faith. He sent me scriptures almost daily to keep me encouraged while I continued building my business and nonprofit. At the end of the day, he was not there for me. It was all a facade. I was ghosted. It hurt. It hurt badly. I felt so alone, abandoned, and discouraged. I desired for a partner to rub my back and shoulders and run his fingers through my hair, kiss my forehead, and tell me that I would be okay. I needed to be loved on. Yet, I lay in bed with what seemed like thousands of pillows, talking to God about my loneliness.

A week after my surgery, I was scheduled for a follow-up appointment with the breast surgeon. I could not drive yet, so my middle sister and my brother-in-law came to take me and my mom to the appointment. I was optimistic that I would get good news and move on with my life and leave this horrible chapter behind. My mom and sister went back to the exam room with me. The breast surgeon entered, took a look at my breasts and told me how good everything looked. However, she had a look of concern on her face. She told me that she got the final pathology results back. My heart sank into my stomach.

"I am so sorry, but we were not able to get clean margins, and need to do another surgery," she said. "There was more DCIS in your breast than showed up on imaging."

Was I hearing her correctly? I was paralyzed.

"You didn't get it all?" I asked. "I have to have another

surgery? When?" I could not process anything she said other than I needed to have another surgery. Lord, why? My family and I prayed and believed that this would be a "one and done" surgery and I could move on with my life after this. I stared blankly at her for about two minutes trying to process what she had just told me. She had such a look of disappointment on her face. She told me she looked over that pathology report over and over again and could not believe what she was reading because she had been confident that she had removed all of the cancer.

My whole body began to shake uncontrollably, and I cried out loud. "Oh, Lord, why?" I kept crying out, "Oh, Lord Jesus, please help me. Please help me!" I couldn't stop shaking and crying. Hearing that I still had cancer left in my body and had to have another surgery felt like I was being newly diagnosed all over again. I felt like I was hyperventilating. How could it be that after all of that testing, they didn't find all of the cancer in my breast? I was dumbfounded. The doctor teared up.

"I have to do the surgery," the surgeon said. "I can't leave it—I just can't leave it."

My mom and sister stood at my side and tried to console me. My middle sister had tears in her eyes. I was breaking my family's heart all over again. It was tearing me up inside. The doctor came to my side, held my hand, and began to pray a powerful prayer over me. We were all in tears after the prayer.

Once I regained my composure, I looked at the doctor.

"It's not your fault," I said. "You are a great surgeon, but this is just a part of the journey that I have to complete." I asked more questions about how soon I could schedule surgery.

"As soon as you would like," she said.

Once the appointment was over, I was scheduled to see the plastic surgeon whose office was just on the other side of the hospital. My family and I walked to the plastic surgeon's office in silence. I was walking and crying. There was nothing anyone could say to make me feel better. I arrived at the office early. We sat in the lobby. The receptionist said that he was in surgery but would be in time for my appointment. My sister and I went to the bathroom. I was still crying. I hugged her and said, "I can't believe this is happening. It all feels like a bad dream." We went back to the waiting room. My middle sister had called my oldest sister and my dad and told them what happened. I didn't want to talk on the phone as I was still shell-shocked from the news. Besides, I didn't know what words to say.

The nurse came to get me for the appointment. My mom and sister accompanied me to the exam room. My mind was still racing. I sat on the exam table with my head held down, shaking my head in disbelief. The plastic surgeon entered. He had a look of genuine compassion and concern. He told me he had already spoken to the breast surgeon about my pathology results. He asked me if I wanted to proceed with a mastectomy or another lumpectomy to try to obtain clear margins. I had become comfortable with the fact that I had smaller breasts and still had my natural nipples and breast tissue. I told him I wanted to proceed with a second lumpectomy to try to get clean margins first and avoid a mastectomy if possible. He explained to me how my current incisions would be opened back up for the surgery and that he would reshape the breast once the breast surgeon had finished her part of the surgery. He also told me he recommended waiting two to three more weeks before surgery to allow the tissues to heal a bit more because I did have a significant amount of swelling in the left breast and chest wall.

When the appointment was over, we headed home. I felt like an animal with my head down and tail tucked between my leg. I felt so defeated. I just knew the first surgery would take care of everything. All I could think about was having to delay returning to work and getting my life back. I got in the car and rode home in silence. I got home, ate in silence, even though my mom was sitting at the table with me, went upstairs, pulled the covers over my head, and slept. I wanted to forget the whole day had even happened.

That weekend, my mom called her sisters who lived in the Atlanta area to let them know she was in town. We did not want them to know that I had surgery because I was still not ready to tell anyone else I had breast cancer, especially now that I had to have a second surgery and did not know how the outcome would be. One of my aunts invited us over for Sunday dinner. I had not driven since surgery and was only one week post-op, and I did not want anyone to see me in pain and with limited range of motion in my arm. I knew that if I looked like I was in pain, people would ask questions. I thought about it for a while, and then thought it would be good for my mom and me to get out of the house for a while. I needed a change of scenery instead of being in bed depressed. We went to my aunt's house, and I actually did not feel bad driving. It made me feel better that I could now drive without a lot of pain. However, I still had to prop a pillow underneath my left arm and put a pillow to cushion my chest for comfort. Nobody noticed anything and my mom and I did not say anything about my surgery. Later in the year, I found out that my uncle had been diagnosed with prostate cancer and had just completed radiation right after I had surgery. He had a history of heart bypass surgery, so was not a candidate for prostate surgery and did not need chemotherapy, therefore radiation was the treatment of choice. Nobody said anything at dinner. Here we were, two family members both fighting cancer at the same time and didn't know it. My aunt told my mom that they just needed to get through it before telling anyone else. I completely understood where she was coming from as I was not yet ready to disclose my diagnosis to the rest of the family for some time. My mom said she had known about it before I did but did not want to tell me and make me worried because I was also dealing with cancer. To top it off, I also found out that one of my aunts was diagnosed with lung, stomach, and uterine cancer and was not doing well. She was my aunt by marriage on my mom's side. My aunt was always so sweet and always called me Cookie. It seemed like no matter how much I tried, I could not escape the big "C" word. It was all around me, swallowing my mind, body, and thoughts.

I had to have a come-to-Jesus meeting with myself before I continued to spiral out of control. I thought to myself, I know my case is different from the norm, but it's not about me. I said to God, "Maybe You are trying to teach my doctors something through my case so that they will know how to respond to this type of situation if they ever encounter it again. Maybe You are teaching them to be better medical providers through me." My pain was being used for a purpose. I had no choice but to be okay with that.

# 19

## The Aftermath

I FELT THAT I WAS RECOVERING PRETTY WELL FROM surgery. I was able to regain range of motion and use of my right arm fairly quickly. About two weeks after surgery, trying to move my left arm became extremely painful. Every time I lifted my left arm past shoulder level, it felt like something was ripping and tearing in my armpit extending down into my tricep. It dawned on me that I was experiencing axillary cording, which is a condition that women commonly get after having breast surgery and lymph node removal. Axillary cording is thought to be scar tissue formed from lymphatic vessels after having lymph nodes removed. Damn, it was painful! Now I knew what my patients felt when they had cording! The beauty of the situation was that because I specialized in cancer rehab, I knew how to treat it. I began aggressively performing more exercises for my left arm, even though I was in tears. I kept telling myself, "You need full use of this arm to get back to work," so I tortured myself through the pain and kept pushing. I would make a conscious effort to use my left arm to reach overhead for something as simple as opening the window blinds in my home. I still had to be careful not to pull my incisions open. I noticed that underneath my left breast there was an open spot that was slow to heal. I didn't want to even think about needing wound care or a possibly infected wound. I thought about how we quickly take for granted the full use and function of our extremities and the natural ability of the body to heal itself until something goes wrong.

After two weeks of caring for me at home, my mom needed to get back home. She had health issues and I did not want her to cancel or miss her important doctor's appointments—even though she wanted to cancel them. I was now able to drive and do light things around my home, so I felt comfortable with her going home. A few weeks before, I had received an invitation to speak at a cancer support group led by a medical oncologist. My friend had been invited to the group and told me that she would let the doctor know that I couldn't make it if I felt that I couldn't do it. Without hesitation, I told her I would go. Besides, I needed to get out of the house because I was going stir crazy.

At the support group, several patients shared their cancer stories. I was tasked with speaking to the group briefly about breast cancer rehab and lymphedema. When it was my turn to speak, I thought, "I am not going through all of this with breast cancer for nothing. It's now or never. Time to speak out about it." I opened up about being diagnosed with breast cancer and having surgery two weeks ago. I shared with the group about how if I was not a physical therapist who specialized in cancer rehab and lymphedema treatment, I would have had to see a physical therapist to restore use of my left arm due to axillary cording. I shared with them about being at risk for developing lymphedema because I had four lymph nodes removed from my left axilla. I also shared about my nonprofit and the book I wrote called, *The Elements of Cancer Survivorship: A Guide to Navigating the Journey*. Someone said, "I would never have known that you had surgery by just looking at you."

After the group session was over, I was approached by several people wanting to inquire more about cancer rehab and how to go about receiving services. Interestingly, I was also approached by one staff member and the director of a breast care center. She said, "As you were speaking, I thought you are exactly who we need, *and* you experienced a breast cancer diagnosis!" She informed me that the breast center was looking to expand and break ground on a new building, and they needed help establishing a lymphedema treatment program at the facility. She asked for my contact information to set up a meeting later to discuss specifics. I was floored. "Look at God!" Keep speaking your truth and you never know what doors will open up for you. God was already quickly using my pain for a purpose.

There was another interesting development. The group announced toward the end of the meeting that they wanted to form a nonprofit called "Cancer Champions." How ironic I thought. The name they had chosen was so similar to the name of my nonprofit Champions Can! Foundation for Cancer Wellness. I was even asked by the oncologist and other group members for help setting up their nonprofit. I was caught off guard, but I agreed. After thinking about it, I thought about how instead of this group reinventing the wheel, they could become a part of Champions Can! because we needed more hands on deck to carry out our mission. My friend ran the idea by the oncologist, who was excited to set up a meeting and discuss how we could carry this out.

I found out that the earliest surgery date available for my second surgery was March 27. Geez! I had to wait another whole month to have surgery? I will be almost fully healed by that time and would have to have these incisions opened up all over again! I became frustrated at being forced to wait. I knew I was not going to be able to get back to work in six to eight weeks as I originally anticipated. While I was waiting to receive my second surgery, I still had some unanswered questions. I wanted to speak with my breast surgeon again for clarity to get more specifics about the second surgery. The office told me that I needed to schedule an appointment to come to the office to talk to her. I did just that. I went to my appointment alone this time. I needed the time and space to myself to ask what I needed to without the influence of anyone else and time to process the information in my own way and in my own time. She was glad that I came back to talk to her. I asked if I would have to have that god-awful wire placement again. She told me I would not.

"So how will you know that you have gotten all of the cancer this time?" I asked.

She told me that she would send the samples in as frozen sections to the pathologist during surgery and keep removing breast tissue until she received the all-clear. She told me that the plastic surgeon would finish the surgery by reshaping the breast. She said it was a possibility that my left breast would be smaller than the right depending on how much tissue had to be removed. Wow! It took me a minute to wrap my mind around what the second surgery would entail. She was a good surgeon, and I trusted her opinion and judgment. I had to go with the flow.

*20*

---

## Pandemic or Peace?

I INFORMED MY FAMILY OF WHEN MY SECOND SURGERY would be. My mom was prepared to come back to take care of me again as long as I needed. My oldest sister was working and did not think that she would be able to take time off of work because she would just be coming off of her spring break. She was very upset at the idea of not being able to be there for me. I told her that she was there for me when I was initially diagnosed and after my first surgery, and to me, she had done more than enough! I told her God would work it out.

In March 2020, the unthinkable happened. The world as we knew it was facing the coronavirus pandemic because of an ugly virus named COVID-19. Apparently, this highly contagious respiratory virus originated in China and was quickly sweeping its way across the US and other countries. It was said to be airborne as well as spread through droplets emitted during talking, coughing, or sneezing. I began to think, "Did I have this virus when I became ill right before my breast surgery in February?" I definitely had some of the symptoms at the time such as fever, fatigue, chills, and a cough that took me six to eight weeks to get rid of with no help from over-the-counter medications. Stores were flooded with people stocking up on groceries and supplies due to fear of the unknown. Paper towel, toilet tissue, hand sanitizer, and disinfectant cleaning products were flying off the shelves. It was like trying to find a needle in a haystack!

Businesses and establishments were shutting down all over. I was thinking I would be able to start some of my contract work again because I had to wait a whole month before my second surgery. However, with the fear of the virus spreading, my contract company stopped sending training assignments for me to go into people's homes to train them on how to use their lymphedema equipment. Even though I really wanted to get back to work, the world was shutting down and my answer was a big fat NO. My oldest sister called me and told me that the schools were shutting down and that the kids would have to learn from home and the teachers and support staff would be working from home. Ha! She would be able to make it to my second surgery after all! As I mentioned before, the director for a local breast center reached out to me as she promised, and we had a meeting scheduled to discuss details about a week prior to my surgery. Due to everything shutting down, the hospital was not allowing any visitors and we had to postpone the meeting. Dang it! This pandemic was messing up a lot of things! I was looking forward to connecting with her to see what new opportunity would come of it, but it was quickly shot down. She told me that she would reach back out to me once things settled a bit.

As my second surgery date approached, I received a call from the hospital to go over pre-op questions and procedures. I was told that my surgery would be in the same building as the first surgery. I was only allowed to have one visitor with me. My surgery time was at three p.m. with a scheduled arrival time of one p.m. Due to the pandemic, they were encouraging those with preexisting medical conditions to stay home because they were the most susceptible to contracting the virus. That, plus not being able to have visitors, meant that my parents would not be able to be with me. I was okay with it. I wanted them to stay home and be safe. My sister would be able to update them on everything happening during my surgery.

Surgery day came quickly. I was nervous. We got to the surgery center without any trouble. There was hardly any traffic because a lot of businesses were closed, and people were working from home as a result of the pandemic. We entered the surgery center and were given a mask, had our temperatures checked, and sanitized our hands. I went to the check-in area again and waited to be taken back for surgery. My sister was allowed to see me one last time before surgery. We talked and joked until the nurse gave me medicine to relax me and I was drifting in and out of sleep. I was escorted to the OR and assisted onto the table. The bright lights were glaring above me. I saw my breast surgeon to my left.

"Let's do this again!" she said.

I woke up in recovery, compression bra intact and bandages and clothes on. The breast surgeon told my sister that they were not able to tell if they were getting clear margins during surgery because the pathologist findings kept coming back as inconclusive. I had to have another follow up with her one week post-op to get the final pathology results. I felt like it was a shot in the dark. The plastic surgeon was able to close up the non-healing area I had under my left breast during surgery with stitches versus using a skin glue that was used for closure during the first surgery. Overall, I did not have as much pain as I did during the first surgery. When we got home, it was after eight p.m. I sat up, ate, and talked to my sister for a while. She called my middle sister and parents to update them on how I was doing. Afterward, I took pain meds and went to bed.

I felt pretty good waking up the next morning. I was able to bathe and dress myself. I looked at my breasts and noticed that my left breast was noticeably smaller than the right, even with all of the swelling. I didn't like the fact that it was smaller, but I had to deal with it. My sister made breakfast and we sat and talked and laughed. In fact, I was feeling so good that we turned on hip-hop and R&B music and I was dancing around my living room. Talk about some good pain meds! My sister thought it was hilarious and caught it all on video. It was amazing that I was laughing and smiling and remaining positive even though I had pending pathology results. After she worked on the computer during the day, we spent the afternoons binge watching TV shows. We watched one particular documentary about the life of a zookeeper and his obsession with tigers. It was very entertaining to think that people actually live that way in real life! Nonetheless, it helped to take my mind off of the medical situation looming over my head. We were also glued to the news for updates on the coronavirus pandemic. I was very fortunate to have my surgery when I did because hospitals were ordered to stop all outpatient elective surgeries in order to preserve personal protective equipment (PPE) for frontline hospital workers. Watching the updates was very alarming. Everybody was encouraged to wear facemasks. If you didn't have one, the surgeon general made commercial campaigns about how to make one out of cloth at home. Georgia mandated stay at home orders. The streets were empty, and more businesses were shutting down. I thought to myself that this gave me more time to recover and was grateful for the downtime. My sister and parents had to support me financially. I was not yet able to go back to work and did not want to burn through my savings. I hated having to ask them for help, but they did their best and got me through it. The last thing I wanted to do was to be a burden on anybody. It was a horrible situation to be in. I had always prided myself on being financially stable and independent, and here I was having to have help from my parents and sister. I should have been taking care of my parents; they shouldn't be taking care of me. I was a grown woman. I was established! All I can say is God humbled me down quickly.

Unfortunately, I was denied financial assistance from the hospital where I initially had my scans and they wanted their money quick, fast, and in a hurry. Medical bills did not stop rolling in and my insurance company was still processing many of the claims that came in. They did set me up with a payment plan, which made it more manageable but financially things were still tight. Due to the pandemic, I was able to suspend my car insurance payments, car payments, credit card payments, and mortgage payments for a while. It was a huge help. After a week, I was doing very well and told my sister it was okay for her to go home. She missed her husband and also needed to get back home to handle some business. Besides, I was used to being home alone and wanted to finish recovering with some quiet time. She didn't want to leave, but I insisted that I would be okay. She knew I had a follow-up appointment coming up, but I told her that I would be fine and let her know as soon as the appointment was done.

The day of my appointment arrived. I prayed and asked God to give me strength, no matter the outcome. I was still working on restoring range of motion in my left arm and had applied elastic taping to my chest, lateral left trunk, and left arm to help with the swelling. I waited for my breast surgeon in the exam room. I tried to read her facial expression, but I couldn't really tell if she had good news or bad news. She examined me first. She saw all of the elastic taping I had on my body and said, "You did this to yourself?"

"Yes," I said, and that I was trying to move the swelling out quickly to help my recovery. Again, the skills I had as a physical therapist were paying off. She was impressed with the amount of range of motion I had regained in my left arm. I expressed to her how I was disappointed with my left breast being significantly smaller than the right, but she assured me that my breasts still looked good.

All right, down to the nitty-gritty. She gave it to me straight, no chaser. She told me that the final pathology came back still showing cancer cells in the margins. However, there was "frank involvement." What in the world did that mean? She broke it down and said there was still a tiny bit left. This was another blow. I took deep breaths and took the time to ask questions. I asked her what my options were. She said I could do radiation, but radiation is usually never performed unless there are clean margins. She said the only other option was to have a mastectomy. If I did not have another surgery, I risked the remaining cancer cells growing again and spreading. She also said that she has had women who have had advanced stages of breast cancer who opted to do nothing other than "a watch and see" approach. Hmmm. I recognized the seriousness of what I was hearing. My body had already been through two surgeries and I did not want to go through another one just yet. My body needed to rest, and I wanted to get back to work. She told me it was completely my choice and to think about it, but in the meantime, she wanted to refer me to a medical oncologist to discuss hormone therapy. I asked her who she liked to refer and, coincidentally, she gave me the name of the medical oncologist who had spoken at my nonprofit event.

I also followed up with the plastic surgeon. He apologized to me again about everything that I had gone through and said that whatever surgery I decided to have, he supported my decision, just to let him know when I was ready. I told him I had an appointment coming up with the oncologist to discuss being placed on hormonal therapy.

"Hormonal therapy can be a game-changer," he said. "It can stop the cancer from growing or shrink it down completely."

I left the appointment with more to think about.

I called my family to update them on, yet again, what I felt was not news I wanted to hear, but for some reason, an unexplainable peace came over me. I was okay with the decision to forego any other surgery for now and to meet with the oncologist. I knew I would have breast imaging again in six months. I was willing to take the chance to see what would happen.

Before my appointment with the oncologist, I decided to go ahead and do the genetic testing. I had to fill out sheets and sheets of my family's medical history. The genetic testing was looking for the BRCA-1 and BRCA-2 genetic mutations. Having these genes meant that a woman has a 50 percent higher risk of developing breast cancer at some point in her life compared to a woman without these genes. This was typically done after an initial diagnosis of breast cancer to help guide treatments. However, my case was not the norm, and I did the genetic testing after the fact. My insurance did not cover it, so I paid $200. I had a long conversation with the genetic counselor. Upon receiving my results, I did not have the BRCA-1 or BRCA-2 mutations. It is so strange to me that there are several women in my family with breast cancer, but of the ones that I asked, none had the genetic mutation. Was there still something familial occurring that had not yet been discovered? Was my breast cancer caused by environmental factors? Was it stress-induced? I did have a very stressful 2019, the year in which my mammogram showed a change. I didn't know the answers, but I did know that Black women are 42 percent more likely than other women to die of breast cancer, and it was becoming an epidemic in the Black community. I had to keep speaking out about it through my nonprofit work.

I went to my appointment with my medical oncologist. She was surprised to see me in her office.

"My goodness, Crystal. I was looking at your file, and I just couldn't believe it," she said.

"Yes, I know," I answered. "It's so ironic that I am the one teaching and preaching to others about cancer rehab and lymphedema, and then I get diagnosed."

She did a physical exam on me.

"Your surgeons did a really good job," she said. "Your breasts look great!"

She didn't seem to notice that my left one was smaller than my right one. It may have been due to me lying down and her angle of view. I sat back up on the table. She told me she saw the results of my final pathology report and saw that I still did not have completely clear margins after the second surgery. Just as I asked all of my other doctors, I asked her, "If you were me, what would you do?"

She stared at me for a moment, and then asked, "Do you want to have children and breast feed?"

"I am not married or dating," I said, "so children are not at the front of my mind. I have had thoughts about what to do. For now, I need to worry about getting my health in order and cross that bridge when I get there."

She stared at me again for a moment and said, "I would do a mastectomy. It is better to do it before the end of the year while your insurance deductibles are met because it will be cheaper for you."

Ugh, I didn't want to think about my insurance company because they were dragging their feet on my claims.

We went on to discuss hormone therapy which she recommended I take a twenty-milligram dose daily for five years. I really did not want to take the medication, which is the hormone therapy of choice for pre-menopausal women who have breast cancers that are estrogen or progesterone positive. It works by blocking cells in the body from responding to estrogen, therefore preventing breast cancer cells from feeding and growing. It was proven to reduce the chance of breast cancer recurrence by 50 percent and also offered protection for the other breast. Again, my breast cancer was 99 percent estrogen positive. I had done my research, and I knew that the medication could have side effects including increased risk for cervical or uterine cancer in addition to many other side effects. I talked to one of my board members for my foundation who was taking the same medication and she described how she had significant side effects, especially hot flashes. I also saw that women who take this medication should not get pregnant. We circled back to the issue of having children in the future. I expressed this concern to my oncologist. She said she could refer me to a reproductive endocrinologist and asked me if I had considered freezing my eggs. I really did not want to freeze my eggs. I had researched it and it was not cheap. Plus, I was already thirty-eight years old and not getting any younger and pretty much had accepted the fact that if it was meant for me to get married and have children, then it would happen when it was supposed to happen naturally. Besides, after five years of being on this medicine, that would put me at forty-three years old, which meant a higher-risk pregnancy. She did tell me that the medication did not affect fertility. If I wanted to get pregnant, I had to stop taking it for six months to a year to avoid effects on the fetus.

Ugh, my head was spinning. I had to do what was best for me at the present time. Since I didn't do radiation and was opting not to do another surgery, deep down something was tugging my spirit, telling me I should proceed with the hormone therapy. I tried to avoid it. I asked the doctor if there were any natural alternatives to the drug. She said that she would not recommend it because the medication suggested had been highly researched and its effectiveness had been proven. I agreed to take the medication. She wrote a prescription and drew blood for labs.

"Follow back up with me in one month," she said, "so I can check on how you are doing with the hormone therapy."

That was it.

I started the hormone therapy and noticed that for some reason I was extremely tired. I wasn't sure if it was from the medicine or trying to get back to work and into the full swing of things. I had returned to work and was taking the necessary precautions to keep myself safe and to protect my patients in the environment of COVID-19. At my one-month follow-up with the oncologist, I told her I was experiencing fatigue and noticed that my menstrual cycle was delayed.

"You aren't pregnant, are you?" she asked.

"My God, no!" I said and laughed.

"Whew," she said, "because you know you aren't supposed to get pregnant while receiving hormone therapy." She also notified me that all of my lab results were normal. "If you feel that you have any issues, please follow back up with me, otherwise I will see you in a year."

That was it. Several days later, my menstrual cycle started. I knew I had to adjust to the medication. I also started taking holy communion every morning and praying before I took the medicine. I prayed that it would do what it was supposed to do without any side effects.

I grew up in a Baptist church and always knew the importance of holy communion. At this point in my life, I could really say I understood the true power of communion and what it represented. I had faith in God to heal me, regardless of what those pathology reports said.

## 21

## Pre-Existing or Just Existing?

BEING A NEW BUSINESS OWNER CAME WITH MANY financial responsibilities. Having to find my own health insurance was one of them. At the time I started my practice, I was healthy with no medical issues. I only went to the doctor for preventative care and screenings. Health insurance plans through the government healthcare marketplace were expensive, so I attempted to cut corners to save money. A colleague connected me with a health insurance broker who went over with me health insurance plans through the marketplace as well as other non-traditional health insurance plans. I decided to go with a short-term medical plan that had a high deductible but covered me at 100 percent for catastrophic events and other basic medical needs. In retrospect, this was a very bad idea! As a healthcare professional, I should have known better, but I felt that I made the best decision for myself at the time.

I did not realize that after reaching the first $5,000 of my $10,000 deductible, that any claims submitted underwent a manual medical review of my medical history for the five years preceding the start of coverage of my insurance plan. Anything in the past five years would be considered a pre-existing condition and would not be covered by this plan, unlike the Obamacare plans through the marketplace in which pre-existing conditions were covered. I should have known something was up when my plastic surgeon's office tried to get authorization from my insurance company for the breast surgery and reconstruction procedure that I originally wanted. They informed the office that they would not give authorization and that all medical claims would have to be submitted first for review before the claims being paid. Ugh! This was very frustrating, but I still knew God was in control and preventing me from undergoing such a drastic surgery such as a double mastectomy with DIEP flap tissue reconstruction, which would have been a much longer recovery for me versus the lumpectomy and oncoplastic reduction. I looked over my health insurance plan documents again and again before starting my breast care and after I received my care. Breast cancer surgery, reconstruction, prosthesis, radiation, and chemotherapy, and any other services and/or procedures related to breast cancer were all listed as covered services under my plan, so I was not worried.

I kept receiving calls from the hospitals and doctor's offices in which I received my breast cancer care stating that my claims had not yet been paid. I informed them that the insurance company was performing a medical review that could take up to sixty days, so the hospitals and offices made notes on my accounts to not send me medical bills to collect payment until the review was completed. After what seemed like forever receiving phone calls urging me to find what the delay was in processing my claims, I received a letter in the mail from the insurance company. The letter stated:

> Dear Ms. Champion,
> We have completed our review of your file.
> Your coverage became effective November 26, 2019. Pre-existing conditions are not covered under your certificate. Your plan states:

*A pre-existing condition means in part a condition:*

*(A) For which medical advice, diagnosis, care, or treatment was recommended or received within the twelve months immediately preceding the date the covered person became insured under the policy;*
*(B) That had manifested itself in such a manner that would have caused an ordinarily prudent person to seek medical advice, diagnosis, care, or treatment within the twelve months immediately preceding the date the covered person became insured under the policy.*

*The policy further states that we will not pay benefits under the policy for a loss which manifests due to, results from, is caused or otherwise contributed to by, a pre-existing condition, or complications resulting from a pre-existing condition.*

*During the course of reviewing your file, medical records were requested and received from [various medical providers]. To assist us in determining whether or not your claims were for pre-existing conditions, we had your medical records reviewed by a qualified doctor. A copy of the doctor's opinion is enclosed with the doctor's name omitted for confidentiality purposes.*

*Based on the medical history, the qualified doctor was of the opinion:*

- *That you received medical advice, diagnosis, care, or treatment within the twelve months immediately preceding November 26, 2019, for the conditions as listed on the enclosed doctor's opinion.*

*The claims which we have received for those conditions listed on the enclosed doctor's opinion are due to pre-existing conditions as defined by your plan and we are unable to accept liability for any expenses incurred for these conditions unless occurring twelve months after the effective date of your policy.*

> *Unrelated conditions will be processed for available benefits.*
>
> *We hereby reserve all of our rights under the policy; specifically those set forth under the Pre-existing Conditions provision and the Reservation of Other Rights provision.*
>
> *If you wish to appeal our decision, please send your written request to [the address for the grievance administrator].*
>
> *You may have additional appeal rights available in your state which have previously been provided to you. Please contact our office if you have any questions.*
>
> *Sincerely,*<br>*[Medical History Review Specialist]*

My heart sank to my stomach. "You have got to be kidding me!" What in the world kind of tomfoolery was this?! I screamed after reading the letter. My head was spinning and pounding at the same time. I began to panic. All the medical care I received for my breast cancer diagnosis amounted to well over $100,000 and they sent me a letter stating my breast cancer was a pre-existing condition and would not be covered? How could that be? I obtained the medical plan with an effective date of coverage beginning November 26, 2019, and did not receive a breast cancer diagnosis until the end of December 2019. Their argument was that the screening mammogram I had on November 5, 2019, that showed new calcifications in my left breast was a condition that would have caused an ordinary person to seek further treatment, which ultimately was considered a pre-existing condition. There was no way that I could pay for all of those medical claims out of pocket! I immediately decided I would appeal the decision. I did some research online about my situation being considered pre-existing. I stumbled across a case report of an Atlanta attorney who had the same health insurance plan when she was transitioning between jobs and was diagnosed with breast cancer after obtaining her plan. The company also denied all of her claims, which amounted to over $300,000 in medical bills. She sued the company, and the case was ruled in her favor and her breast cancer medical claims were paid. "Jesus, Jesus!" I said. "I have enough going on. I definitely don't have time to enter a legal battle with a health insurance company!"

I was really hoping and praying I wouldn't have to go to these lengths. I was already dealing with enough. It seemed like I kept falling deeper and deeper into a hole. When was it going to end?

Not only that, about a month before my breast cancer diagnosis, I had reached out to an insurance broker to obtain additional life and disability insurance. They reviewed my medical records, and I was denied based on the cancer diagnosis. Being self-employed, I needed those benefits! Luckily, I already had another life insurance policy that I purchased several years ago.

I attempted to reach out to the client that was mentioned in the case. She was now practicing law in Atlanta. I wanted to pick her brain about her case and see if there were any pointers she could help me with for the appeals process. I made several attempts to reach her office and left numerous voicemails and emails without a response back. Now what was I going to do?

I reached out to my breast surgeon and plastic surgeon and informed them of the situation. They were both shocked and appalled. They both wrote letters for me not only to support my request for an appeal but also to confirm the dates of when I first came to see them for treatment, which was well after the effective date of coverage for my insurance plan.

The letter I wrote was as follows:

> *Dear Grievance Administrator,*
>
> *I am writing this letter due to a correspondence I received via mail from you, dated May 4, 2020, and stating that I am denied medical coverage benefits due to a pre-existing condition. My member ID is [xxxxxxxxx]. The claims affected include the following dates of service:*
> *–12/05/2019*
> *–12/23/2019*
> *–1/06/2020*
> *–1/07/2020*
> *–1/10/2020*

–1/30/2020
–2/17/2020
–2/18/2020
–3/13/2020
–3/27/2020
–4/2/2020
–4/20/2020
–5/15/2020

*Your correspondence states that my breast cancer is a pre-existing condition. The start of my plan policy was 11/26/2019. I did not officially receive a confirmed diagnosis of left breast ductal carcinoma in-situ, confirmed by biopsy and pathology report, until after the effective date of my plan policy. Otherwise, I had a standard routine screening mammography on 11/05/2019 and at that time, no diagnosis was made, and I did not exhibit any signs or symptoms of breast cancer.*

*Please see the attached documentation from my [breast surgeon and my plastic surgeon]. These physicians treated me for breast cancer, and they support and confirm the medical necessity of the treatment I received, the dates of initial consultation, the date of a confirmed breast cancer diagnosis, and supporting medical records that my breast cancer was not a pre-existing condition. Having a family history of breast cancer and undergoing a routine "screening" mammography is not a condition or a diagnosis or diagnostic conclusion.*

*I am requesting an appeal and a review of the case. Please accept this letter and supporting documentation as my request for an appeal of the adverse determination and as a request to have my medical records reviewed to have my medical claims paid for my breast cancer treatment. Please reconsider your decision as the denial of my claims are very financially taxing at this time, amounting to over $100,000 in medical debt. Thank you for your consideration.*

*Kindest Regards,*
*Crystal Champion*

The letter from my breast surgeon was as follows:

*To Whom It May Concern:*

*I am writing this letter on behalf of Ms. Crystal Champion, who I have had the pleasure of caring for since January 2020. It has come to my attention that her medical benefits and coverage for management of her breast cancer care are being denied due to the belief that this is a pre-existing condition.*

*Ms. Champion changed her insurance coverage and solicited your business in November 2019. Please allow me to lay out a timeline of her care to make it very clear that Ms. Champion's diagnosis was NOT pre-existing, nor would she willingly or knowingly take advantage of an already delicate and overworked healthcare system.*

*Timeline of Events:*

- *November 2019: Coverage with [your company]*
- *November 5, 2019: yearly screening mammogram performed*
- *Of note, Ms. Champion has an extensive and significant family history of breast cancer and has been receiving yearly screening mammograms since 2018*
- *Screening mammogram deemed suspicious and additional views recommended for further evaluation*
- *December 5, 2019: Left breast diagnostic views performed, and left breast calcifications are highly suspicious for possible malignancy. Stereotactic core biopsy performed.*
- *January 6, 2020: Stereotactic core biopsy performed*
- *January 7, 2020: Core biopsy pathology resulted and demonstrated ductal carcinoma in situ.*
- *Please note that this is the actual diagnosis date.*
- *January 10, 2020: First consultation with my office.*

> Recommendation made for a total mastectomy or an extensive wide local excision
> - Referral made to plastic surgeon to discuss reconstruction options
> - February 18, 2020: operative procedure
> - March 27, 2020: Subsequent return to the operating room required in conjunction with plastic surgeon.
>
> Please find attached supporting documents, including radiology reports, pathology reports with dates in full view, and operative reports supporting that Ms. Champion did NOT have a breast cancer diagnosis (i.e. pre-existing condition) at the time of commencement of her medical coverage in November.
> Thank you for your detailed attention to this matter as I continue to care for Ms. Champion and others who deserve top-notch care.
> If there are questions, concerns, or additional information needed to resolve this matter, please do not hesitate to reach out to me directly.
>
> Sincerely,<br>[Breast Surgeon]

The letter from my plastic surgeon read as follows:

> To Whom It May Concern:
> Ms. Champion is a thirty-eight-year-old female that was diagnosed with left breast DCIS by [her breast surgeon]. She presented to our office on 1/22/2020 for a consultation regarding immediate breast reconstruction following a planned mastectomy. The surgical procedures were discussed and explained to the patient involving possible risks, complications, and planned approach. On 2/18/2020 the patient underwent a left oncoplastic breast reduction (wise pattern, inferior pedicle flap) and right balancing breast reduction. We recently received a denial from the

*patient's health plan citing pre-existing health conditions. Please note that this patient was not seen for this condition prior to her first scheduled appointment with our office on 1/22/20. I have attached supporting medical records to this letter. Please do not hesitate to contact my office if you need additional information.*

*Sincerely,*
*[Plastic Surgeon]*

I was so blessed to have doctors who responded quickly to my request for their help and were willing to go to bat for me. I submitted their letters along with the letter that I wrote to the insurance company to begin the appeals process. I contacted the insurance company to let them know that I would be sending in information to request an appeal and they informed me that it could take sixty days to review my file to make a decision.

I packaged up the materials, prayed over them, and mailed them off. In the meantime, I reached out to other local attorneys that specialized in healthcare claims for consultations. I was pretty much advised that I had to go through the Georgia grievance process of appeals first before I could take other legal action. That was such a slap in the face. I had to play the waiting game. I applied for financial assistance from the two hospitals in which I received care. One denied me, stating my income level was too high, so I was placed on a payment plan. The other hospital informed me that after submitting an application, that it could take thirty to sixty days for approval.

The phone calls kept coming because these hospitals and medical practices wanted their money *expeditiously*. I had bills from hospitals, general labs, pathology labs, radiology, anesthesiology, the breast surgeon, the plastic surgeon, and the oncologist. Month after month the bills were piling up. I was constantly on the phone notifying all of them that the claims were denied, and I was in the process of an appeal. I was doing this to try to put the bills on hold as much as possible. I was so afraid I would be sent to collections. I was afraid that I would have to file bankruptcy to get away from it all. I always prided myself on paying my bills on time and having an excellent credit score. Dealing with breast cancer was causing me to face the possibility of financial ruin. I was in disbelief. Here I was, a medical professional and facing all of this mental and financial stress due to a breast cancer diagnosis, something I see my patients deal with every day.

I even attempted to apply for financial assistance from some of the other cancer support organizations in the area. Of course, they always looked at income, and I repeatedly received the same slap-in-the-face answer that I didn't qualify for assistance because I made "too much" money. Here I was, slowly starting to treat patients again, still trying not to blow through my savings, and I couldn't get financial assistance. In my mind, regardless of your income, if you need help, you need help!

Ironically, at the time I was dealing with all of my insurance woes, I was also in the process of restructuring the financial assistance program of my nonprofit organization. After the experience I had with trying to obtain financial support, I made it a point to take off income requirements for people in need. I now knew what it felt like and I surely did not want anyone else to have to experience what I was experiencing. I knew there were people in much worse situations than myself. Maybe that was what God was trying to get me to see in a much different light. "Okay, God, I get it! You have shown me enough!"

Unfortunately, my appeal to the insurance company was denied. They were still saying that my breast cancer was a pre-existing condition. I was beyond frustrated, nervous, anxious, and upset. In the political realm, the country was in the middle of campaigns for who would be the next president of the United States. Healthcare was amongst various issues that were brought up. I was sickened to my stomach to hear that the current administration wanted to take away protections for pre-existing medical conditions. Here I was going through it as a cancer patient. It hurt my heart to the core to think about other cancer patients who could potentially lose coverage and also be stuck with astronomical medical bills or who may even have to forego medical care altogether because they simply could not afford to pay for the numerous appointments, scans, lab tests, chemotherapy, and radiation. This was playing with people's lives! I calmed myself down by recalling the dream that I had after I had just been diagnosed with breast cancer, the one where I was on the back of a truck, unable to see the driver, but riding through a storm, ultimately surviving unscathed and untouched. I cried out to God and said, "God, you promised me that you would take care of me through all of this, and I am calling on you and depending on you to fulfill your promise to me!"

After about another month of trying to set up payment plans with all of the people I owed and trying to pay as much as I could to avoid being sent to collections as threatened on several of my billing statements, I received a letter from the second hospital that I applied to for financial assistance. The letter stated that I was approved for 95.5 precent forgiveness! The letter also stated that it could be applied to future services as well as other ancillary services received that were a part of the hospital system but only at the determination of those other providers that I received services from. I cried tears of joy and felt a huge wave of relief! I was able to send the letter to my breast surgeon, plastic surgeon, and other ancillary services received who all honored my financial assistance letter and adjusted my account balances accordingly. I even started receiving checks in the mail for overpayments after the accounts were adjusted. I thought for sure that my insurance appeal would be granted, and my claims would be paid. However, God had another plan. He did it in a manner that I did not expect, especially after being told over and over again that I did not qualify for financial assistance. God is AMAZING! He told me he would take care of me, and he did. It served as a reminder to me that God always steps in on time. This was an Ephesians 3:20–21 moment:

*Now unto him that is able to do exceeding abundantly above all that we ask or think, according to the power that worketh in us,*

*Unto Him be glory in the church by Christ Jesus throughout all ages, world without end. Amen.*[1]

**God truly is DOPE.**

---

[1] King James Version.

## 22

## Second Quarter 2020—Coming Out

MAY 7, 2020, WAS THE DAY OF MY LIVING BEYOND Breast Cancer interview. The organization reached out to me about facilitating a session regarding managing lymphedema during the coronavirus pandemic. As a reminder, this was the organization in Philadelphia, Pennsylvania, that I was originally going to lead a workshop session for on lymphedema and cancer rehab. I informed the CEO that since my conference attendance in September 2019, I was diagnosed with breast cancer.

"Wow, this is so amazing! You can definitely bring a whole new perspective to the situation," she replied when she heard of my diagnosis. I knew that before I did this interview and put it out for the world to see, I had to share my journey with breast cancer with those who didn't know yet. I was finally at the point where I was ready to tell people outside of my immediate family about what I went through. Nobody knew of my journey except for my mom, my dad, two sisters, two brothers-in-law, and my niece and nephew. Due to the pandemic and not being able to gather together, I had a video call with my oldest sister and two first cousins, who were also my sorority sisters. Not only were they cousins, they were like sisters to me. I didn't want to tell them, but I wanted them to hear about it straight from the horse's mouth versus finding out on social media.

Once my LBBC interview was ready to be released, I made the following social media post:

> *I am so honored to have been chosen by Living Beyond Breast Cancer to share information about managing lymphedema during the coronavirus pandemic! Being a healthcare provider and now a BREAST CANCER SURVIVOR, yes, A BREAST CANCER SURVIVOR, I am able to help and assist patients in a greater way!*
>
> *This may come as a surprise and a shock to many. Although this is not an easy thing to share, I was diagnosed with Ductal Carcinoma In-Situ (non-invasive early-stage breast cancer) of my left breast in December 2019. I have had two surgeries with sentinel lymph node biopsy (four lymph nodes removed) and I am doing well by the grace of God! I could not have handled this gracefully without my faith in God and the unwavering, loving support from my sisters, parents, and a very close friend/breast cancer survivor, who were the only ones that knew about my diagnosis at the time.*
>
> *This was something that I did not expect, nor a journey I thought that I would ever have to travel being that I work with cancer patients daily and also have a nonprofit organization that supports and advocates for cancer survivorship. However, my work and passion for helping and supporting others prepared me to boldly take that walk into my own personal journey of cancer survivorship.*
>
> *With that being said, I am even more passionate and dedicated to continuing to assist cancer patients through my platforms as a lymphedema therapist and through my nonprofit organization Champions Can! I will share more details of my journey at a later time, but for now I want to*

stress the importance of EARLY DETECTION! Listen to your body and those inner promptings if you feel that something is not right. Do not put off getting your yearly check-ups and exams. To my women, GET YOUR YEARLY MAMMOGRAMS! If you have a history of breast cancer in your family, DO NOT WAIT until you are age forty before receiving your first mammogram. I am thirty-eight years old and have always advocated for my health and was diligent about getting my yearly check-ups. If I had waited until I was forty to receive my first mammogram, we may be having a different discussion right now.

This is just the beginning and there is definitely more to come! Be safe, be well, be encouraged, remain faithful, and please prioritize your health! #ChampionsCan #BreastCancerSurvivor #Survivorship #Passion #Purpose #ATrueChampion

These are some of the comments I received:

"Wow! Thank you so much for your transparency cousin! I'm so proud of you! God is so faithful! Love you! Continue to use your pain for purpose to be an inspiration!"

"Congratulations and stay beautiful Crystal Champion. May blessings keep coming your way."

"Your resiliency, perseverance, determination, and experiences are going to bless so many. May the Lord continue to bless you as you continue to be a blessing to others. Love you, sis! #GodsGoodness"

"I'm so thankful that God kept you during this time! So brave of you to share your testimony. I love you! #youreasuperwoman"

"I'm in complete shock! I'm so sorry you have to join this club but your strength and faith will carry you far. I'm here for you. I hope you know that. Hugs and love. Xo."

"Thinking of you, Crystal Champion! So glad this was caught early. This will definitely give new meaning and purpose to the wonderful work you do. Hugs!"

"Crystal, I'm speechless but ahhhhmmmaaazzzeeddd at how strong you are, well nah not really you've always held a strength that most of us can only wish we had. I love you and I'm excited to see where your journey takes you."

"So glad you beat it with of course the help of God. He is using you to be more of an inspiration to your patients. You can now relate to them even more."

"I'm so speechless, you're a wonderful person and you were there for me when I needed advice. I admire your strength too and remember we're in this together."

"Hi Crystal, I saw/read your interview on LBBC Instagram. I was shocked when I read that you, too, had breast cancer. I'm so sorry to hear this. You are such a kind, giving person. Not to forget, the best lymphedema therapist ever! I wish you continued positive health."

"What an awesome testament of God's power! Thank you for availing yourself to assist so many who otherwise may not have hope. Super proud of you."

"Glad to hear your recovery my dear. You are definitely a shero. Thanks for educating and creating this awareness to all. So important. Stay blessed and keep the faith sister."

"Dr. Champion, you are a great hero and have always been an inspiration. Right now, I can't think of a better title or label because you are a role model to me. Thank you for sharing this experience of going through and fighting cancer and I am glad to be with you as we are in remission. Hugs and positive vibes. Please, please reach out to me if you want to talk, vent, or anything. I am gladly wanting to be there for you like you been there for me. Not sure if your number changed or if you have mine. Anyway, reach me here or text. Whatever you need. Just let me know."

"Crystal, thank you for sharing your testimony and journey with us. My mind went immediately to God's provisions for us. He always provides what we need, when we need it and how we need it. Great is His faithfulness. Who knew that a pandemic would connect you to Bible study *with your home church and the studies would be just what you needed during this leg of your journey. Who knew? God knew! May this adversity be a bridge to a deeper relationship with God; be an opportunity to encourage, inspire, and bring healing to others. Love you and I am grateful to be a part of your journey . . . love you much!"*

I finally did it! It was a relief to share with others the battle I was secretly fighting. It was empowering to show my vulnerability but also my strength in the face of adversity. The support and encouragement I received made me want to keep working and fighting even harder to help cancer patients and to bring awareness to cancer survivorship. It was more evident why I was diagnosed with breast cancer. God needed me to expand my reach and my platform to help restore healing to people in a greater way.

## 23

## Protests and Prosperity

"BLACK LIVES MATTER! BLACK LIVES MATTER! BLACK Lives Matter!"

"I can't breathe! I can't breathe! I can't breathe!"

Not only were we in the middle of the coronavirus pandemic, but we were also in the middle of civil unrest and protests for a variety of reasons. Watching the news, several Black men and a Black woman were victims of racial injustice, systemic racism, and police brutality.

It started with Ahmaud Arbery, a twenty-five-year-old Black man who was gunned down on February 23, 2020 in broad daylight while jogging by two white men in Brunswick, Georgia; then George Floyd, a forty-six-year-old Black man who died on May 25, 2020, in Minneapolis, Minnesota, while police kneeled on his neck for eight minutes and forty-six seconds; then Rayshard Brooks, a twenty-seven-year-old Black man who was shot and killed in Atlanta, Georgia, by police on June 12, 2020, less than three weeks after the killing of George Floyd; then Breonna

Taylor, a twenty-six-year-old Black woman was shot and killed by white policemen during a botched raid on her apartment in Louisville, Kentucky, on March 13, 2020.

Even in the middle of a pandemic, these events sparked protests across the United States. Waves and droves of people in almost all major cities across the US were protesting. Some protests were peaceful, yet people were still tear-gassed, arrested, and shot with rubber bullets. Some rioting also occurred. Businesses were being burned to the ground and buildings and statues were being defaced. People were angry and fed up. Streets were blocked, and traffic, even on major interstates, was blocked by protestors who were determined to stand in solidarity against the recent events. I dropped my mouth in disbelief as I watched the news unfold at the CNN Center and as other historic landmarks in downtown Atlanta were defaced. Police cars were burning in the streets and smoke and fire plumes lit up the night sky.

I was becoming numb to it all. I watched the videos of those men being murdered and even though it was difficult to watch, I was emotionless. These people were killed like dogs in the street. I didn't know how to feel. I was already emotionally exhausted from dealing with my breast cancer diagnosis, surgeries, and insurance issues. I had no capacity to handle or mentally process what I was seeing and hearing. It was downright frightening. I was forced to think about my own experiences with often being the only Black person in a group or work environment and constantly having to prove myself and my credentials as a Black physical therapist. I thought back to when my oldest sister and I were racially profiled at a dollar store.

I was also reminded of a time when I had to explain to my fellow colleagues why the term "gal" was offensive. One of my white colleagues was working with an older Black woman in her hospital room, providing her physical therapy. Apparently, the woman did a great job during her treatment session, so the white male therapist said to her, "Good job, gal." This did not sit well with the patient, and she was infuriated with the therapist. I remember him sharing this incident with us during lunch break that day. He was so distraught that he had offended this woman and did not understand why. I was tired of holding my tongue and being quiet. Being the only Black person in the room at the time, I had to speak up. "Y'all are gonna learn today," was my first thought. I had to school them. I explained to them that a Black woman being called "gal" was deemed as a derogatory term and basically the equivalent of a Black man being called the "N" word. This went back to times of slavery as well as during the Civil Rights Movement. Some still could not understand why it was so hurtful, even though they frequently used it as a term of endearment toward others. My supervisor at the time chimed in and said very hastily, "People are always getting offended about something." I shook my head in disbelief. Black people are so tired of having to explain ourselves. So tired of trying to prove ourselves. So tired of fighting to be seen. So tired of fighting to be heard. Exhausted from comments about our skin color and how our hair is different while asking, "Can I touch it?" as if we are animals in a damn petting zoo.

My mind couldn't even fathom what these people and their families were going through. The Black community was triggered and hurting. Years and years we have been treated unfairly, yet we have had to suppress our thoughts and our tongues for fear of the backlash or being fired from our jobs or targeted in some other way. Were we living in the 1960s? Were we really as progressive as we thought we were here in this country? What was going on with race relations in our country? Why was so much hate being perpetuated? Why was the Black community being hit so hard with police brutality and hit even harder with racial disparities in our communities and deaths from the coronavirus pandemic? Why were the bodies of Black men still being hung in trees in 2020? Why were nooses still being erected as threats against Blacks . . . in 2020?

In the midst of it all, we lost two great civil rights icons and Freedom Riders on the same day, July 17, 2020: Reverend C. T. Vivian and Congressman John Lewis. We also lost another remarkable leader in the country on September 18, 2020: Supreme

Court Justice Ruth Bader Ginsburg. Collectively, these leaders were tireless champions for justice, and now they were gone as the country was experiencing political and civil upheaval.

While struggling to mentally and emotionally process all of the craziness going on in the country, I had bigger chickens to fry. In addition to the medical bills I was fighting, my therapy practice was going downhill due to the pandemic because patients did not want to come to therapy, nor did they want to pay cash for treatment. My caseload dropped significantly. I still had my contract job, but I needed more than that. Financially, I had to do something before I sunk too far into a hole. I was becoming spiritually and emotionally exhausted.

One day as I was in bed, I received a text message from a former colleague stating that my former rehab supervisor was leaving. I was surprised at the news, which prompted me to go on the hospital's career site to see what positions were open. I was being nosey and wanted to see what was up. I stumbled upon a position for a cancer rehab director for a group of clinics associated with a hospital system. I thought back to how I always said at cancer committee meetings that a position needed to be created to ensure cancer patients were not getting lost in the system and getting what they needed from a rehab standpoint. I had to shoot my shot and apply for the position. Unfortunately, I was a bit late to the party. After about two weeks, I saw that the position had been closed and someone else was hired. The lymphedema therapist who I shadowed before becoming certified was selected for the position. "Wow, really?" I didn't stop there. "What God has for me is for me," I told myself. As I continued my job search, I hoped to find something part-time which would still allow me the time to continue to rebuild my therapy practice. I came across a full-time position for a lymphedema therapist for a new clinic that was a part of another major health system in Atlanta. The clinic's specialty was pelvic floor therapy and lymphedema. *Wow, this is an amazing opportunity*, I thought. I had experience starting a lymphedema program and was also running my own business, so why not use that opportunity to expand my reach and be of service to someone else while also regaining financial security? I had to shoot my shot again and I applied for the position. The very next day, the recruiting manager from the organization said that she had received my application and was very excited that I would be an excellent fit for the position. She told me she would expedite my application and résumé to the hiring managers. Just as she said, the clinic manager reached out to me two days later to schedule a virtual interview. It sucked that I was not able to have an in-person interview to really get a feel for the clinic and staff, but I was grateful to have the chance. The virtual interview with the clinic manager went very well. She was also lymphedema certified. However, she wanted to focus more on the pelvic floor clientele while having another therapist focus solely on the lymphedema population. I was given a virtual tour of this beautiful brand-new clinic with two private treatment rooms, one for each therapist. It was quite a drive from my home, but at that point I was willing to do what was necessary for the position. Two days after that, the clinic manager scheduled me for an interview with both the local rehab manager and regional rehab director for the facility. It turns out that the local rehab manager already knew who I was because she had attended an event in March 2019 that I held for lymphedema awareness month for my nonprofit foundation. She was super excited that we had crossed paths again. I had a lot to think about. The position was full-time, so that meant I would have very little time, if any, to keep my therapy practice going on the side. I was praying and thinking about what to do if offered the position. One day I was en route to see a home client and meditating and praying about this job opportunity. "Lord what do you want me to do?" Right after that, I looked up and saw a billboard for the organization I had applied to. This organization doesn't even have hospitals or clinics on my side of town and as much as I travel the I-85 corridor I have *never* seen a billboard advertising this organization. God had given me a sign as clear as day.

Two days later, I received an offer letter. They wanted to hire me! Who in the world gets hired in the middle of a pandemic? I was watching other medical professionals getting laid off or furloughed, and they wanted me! I accepted the offer, which turned out to be a sweet deal! My therapy practice was my baby, so I second-guessed myself about taking the full-time position and what it would entail. However, God sent me more confirmation that I had made the right decision. A week later, I found out I was laid off from my job as a contract trainer. The company had been hit hard financially due to the pandemic and laid off all lymphedema pump trainers. It came without warning in a nice little email that was sent out. Geez! If it ain't one thing it's another! I was so grateful to God that I had taken the position at the new clinic, as my hand would have been forced to do it anyway.

I was given a start date of May 26, 2020, to begin orientation. About a week before orientation, I got a call in the morning from the recruiting manager that first contacted me that the healthcare system was furloughing employees due to the financial hit from COVID-19, and they were delaying the start date of all new hires until August 17, 2020. The recruiting manager asked me if I was working. I told her I had just been laid off from my contract job and had a limited caseload for my current practice. She apologized to me for the decision and said that she also was blindsided. She told me that she would keep an eye out for me for any PRN positions that became available and send them to me. My heart sank. "Okay, God, I still trust you. What you have for me is for me." I refused to panic about the situation, even though I knew I really wanted and needed to start work soon. Two hours later, I got a call from the regional manager who also apologized about the news and said that they needed me to start working at the clinic on the original start date because they had already begun marketing efforts and were starting to receive referrals at the clinic for lymphedema patients.

"Let me talk to the higher-ups," she said, "and see what I can do. I'm not sure if we will know anything today but I hope to let you know soon." Three hours later, she called me back and said, "You are starting May 26 as planned!"

That door swung wide open for me! I fell to the floor in tears of praise. God is amazing and truly was looking out for me. For all of the loss I endured in 2020, I gained much more. I was now presented with the opportunity to serve more patients on a larger scale. Who knew what this would lead to!

I started receiving more good news. I found out that I was selected to serve as an Elevate Ambassador for the National Coalition for Cancer Survivorship. Additionally, the CEO nominated me to their National Quality Control Council because they needed input from a cancer rehab therapist. I happily accepted! I was selected to serve on the GC3 Advocacy Council for the Georgia Center for Oncology, Research, and Education. The director for a breast imaging center also reached out to me. She apologized for having to cancel our meeting scheduled earlier in the year due to the pandemic, but she wanted me to do a webinar for the breast center staff about lymphedema and breast cancer rehabilitation. I eagerly obliged. After I completed the presentation, she was very grateful and said, "We will definitely be in touch for the future. I still need your help." Not only was I about to touch patients at my new clinic, my platform was also being elevated for my nonprofit organization. I was reminded of John 10:25 (ESV) in which Jesus says, "I told you, and you do not believe. The works that I do in My Father's name, they bear witness of Me." I finally understood what one of my favorite pastors Joel Osteen meant when he said, "God knows how to prosper you, even in a desert."

## 24

## Third Quarter 2020—Taking the "Ls"

I BEGAN THE EFFORT OF TRYING TO HIRE A THERAPIST to help me run my therapy practice although I was working full-time for another organization. Eminence Physical Therapy was my baby. I had poured my all into it, and I wanted to keep it going. A male lymphedema therapist reached out to me a year ago to pick my brain about Eminence PT because he was intrigued by how my business was structured. He later saw a job posting I had for a contract lymphedema therapist and reached out to me again. We scheduled a meeting, and I was ecstatic that he met all of the qualifications I was looking for. We met up and I showed him around the clinic and gave him insight about how my business was structured. This didn't work out due to logistical reasons. He had just taken a part-time job with a home health agency in North Georgia, so coming to help me at my clinic would be difficult due to the location. Another therapist applied that also had the qualifications I was looking for but did not have the availability I needed. I needed someone who could provide services for me as needed 8:00 a.m. to 4:00 p.m., Mondays through Fridays. This was not going the way I had planned AT ALL!

I was telling my oldest sister about my frustrations with being unable to find help.

"Sis, I have to put my big girl panties on, put this ego aside, and let my business go for now," I said. I was very distraught about having to make the decision. I felt like I had failed.

"Sis don't look at it as a failure," she said, encouraging me. "This is your business and your baby. It doesn't have to go anywhere unless you want it to, but for now, I think you should take a step back temporarily and focus on your full-time job. Whenever you do decide to revamp your business, it will be bigger and better!"

I got what she was saying, but it still didn't take the sting off of my ego. Shortly after this conversation, I received an email from a newly certified lymphedema therapist. I was amazed because she was just certified by the same school where I received my certification.

Her email to me was as follows:

> *Good evening Dr. Crystal Champion. My name is [occupational therapist], OTR/L, CLT and I have done quite a bit of research on the many different avenues that I can take in Georgia as a Certified Lymphedema Therapist! I have continuously come across your company site and I am very intrigued. I find your professional and personal story to be very motivating and inspirational. I am reaching out because I would love to learn more about any available opportunities and/or opportunities for future growth within your company! I have attached my résumé. I truly admire your drive and professionalism, and as an African American Woman from Gwinnett County (who is also a Soror) it is refreshing to see a small Black-owned medical business! It would be an honor to chat with you regardless of the open availability to learn more about the business and maybe some hurdles you have experienced. Please feel free to reach out to my email or via phone anytime at your convenience! I look forward to hearing from you!*

I hadn't considered hiring an OT or someone newly trained because I was already extremely overwhelmed. I was forced to see patients from 5:30 p.m. or later after having already worked eight hours at my new full-time job, so I was exhausted. I would wake up at 5:00 a.m. and not get home until 8:00 p.m. I felt it was my job to steer this new therapist in the right direction. I reached out to her and allowed her to come and shadow me while treating patients. She was amazed at all that I was doing and still trying to do with my business and excited to come on board to help me. I was burning the candle at both ends and I could tell it was beginning to take a toll on me physically. "Stress causes cancer, and I'm definitely not trying to do that again," I told myself. I had to switch gears for my health and my sanity.

After much more thought and consideration, I had to keep it real with myself. I knew deep down that I did not have the time to properly train this therapist and mentor her in the manner in which she needed to be able to grow and gain experience. Trying to hire a therapist was just not working out, and I had to be okay with it. I sent her the following email:

> *Hi Soror! Hope things are well!*
>
> *After much tough deliberation and re-evaluating my business structure, I have decided not to move forward with adding on a new team member at this time. This definitely does not mean I will not want to bring you on as a team member in the future. I will actually be closing down my Snellville office and doing a complete restructure and potential location change versus staying mobile. I do want to however point you in the direction of some lymphedema positions that are open in the Atlanta area that you may be interested in to gain some experience and maybe transition into treating lymphedema part-time or full-time. I found some openings at [another hospital]. See the link below and I definitely encourage you to apply! You have a passion and drive to do lymphedema and learn more and I honestly feel that working in a hospital facility will give you lots of*

experience very fast! Treating lymphedema in a hospital setting truly helped me to prepare for launching my own business. I am always here for you to answer questions or to mentor you in any way that I can, and please know that I will definitely keep your résumé on hand and you in mind in the future for Eminence PT. Please reach out to me anytime and feel free to call me if you have any questions or just to chat or hang out as Sorors!

Her reply was as follows:

*Good morning Crystal!*

*I am sad to hear this, however, I completely understand as I know times are hard right now. I agree that considering relocation is a great idea and route to go as there are so many more hospitals in the city! I appreciate you looking into that position and I completely agree that it would be best to learn and grow as a Lymphedema therapist in a Hospital. And . . . of course I would love to continue to hang out Soror/Mentor/all that!! Lol. We should definitely grab drinks sometime! You have motivated me beyond what you could imagine in just one session of getting to know you! Please do keep in touch! Have an Awesome day!!*

*Sisterly . . .*

I decided to close down my office. November 30 was my last day. I still had a client I was treating, and we were nearing the end of his treatment. I notified my building owner that I would be moving out at the end of November.

"Well, that is perfect timing!" she said. She informed me that she had finally found someone who wanted to purchase the building, which was put up for sale earlier in the year. She was not certain that the new owners would allow us to continue to rent space from them. I realized whether I wanted to or not, I would have had to close my space anyway. It was like God was moving me in a completely different direction. It became clearer why trying to hire a therapist was not working out. Shortly after I closed my office and finished my last client, I received the following email from the patient's wife:

> Dr. Champion,
>
> I am [the wife of your patient]. I wanted to let you know that he passed away suddenly on December 10 from a heart attack.
>
> We were so shocked of course, and I've been working through all of his personal situations and trying to step up and run the business as well along with our son.
>
> I know that he appreciated all that you did for him and the improvements you were able to make for his quality of life with his ongoing edema. The home unit that he was using was a great help to him. That being said, he only had it for a short time and I was wondering if it might be returned, or if not, is there possibly someone that can use it? Thank you for all you did for [him]. Please feel free to call me if you like.

What! I was in complete shock. I couldn't believe what I was reading! He was one of my loyal customers and had made lots of progress. There was never any indication in his medical history that he had heart issues. Wow, Wow, Wow! Moral of the story: always treat people with kindness and respect because you never know when it will be your last time interacting with them.

## 25

## Vision 2020—Year-in-Review

THE YEAR 2020 WAS DEFINITELY ONE FOR THE HISTORY books, to say the least! It was the year that kept on giving. Even though the year was flying by, it still seemed like it would never end! I continued to have eye-opening experiences. Here is my version of what I call my 2020 year-in-review: We were losing iconic figures in the country all while experiencing a global pandemic. I mentioned earlier about the civil unrest and protests. Unemployment rates were at historic all-time highs and the political ads for the upcoming presidential election were outrageous and out of control. We had a record Atlantic hurricane season with thirty-one named storms. There was a Saharan dust cloud that blanketed portions of the country, a phenomenon that happens every year but was the most significant in 2020. There were also an unprecedented number of wildfires plaguing the western United States. Our country was just in a mess all the way around.

The death of one of my favorite actors was the icing on the cake. On August 28, 2020, Chadwick Boseman passed away from colon cancer. He was only forty-three years old and in the prime of his career. He continued to work and produce high-quality movies all while he was in the fight for his life battling colon cancer. He was an amazing actor. Not to mention I had a huge crush on him. He always showed humility whenever he spoke or was interviewed. I reflect back on February 28, 2018, the day *Black Panther* was released. It displayed nothing but Black excellence! In the midst of the celebration of the movie *Black Panther*, there was also an important message that I felt was being overlooked. Chadwick Boseman has had numerous acting roles and never really received the recognition he deserved. He portrayed Jackie Robinson, James Brown, Thurgood Marshall in addition to other acting roles. He was blessed with the opportunity to make history by portraying a Black superhero in a movie that was breaking records across the country and the world. *Black Panther* was orchestrated tactfully and carried out with dignity and grace, truly highlighting the beauty of my people and the power we truly possess.

The following message has resonated with me: Keep being diligent and faithful where you are. When God gets ready to open doors for you and promote you to the next level, nobody, not even yourself, will even begin to fathom how awesome God is! God will catapult you so far beyond what you could even imagine or think that people will have no choice but to acknowledge that it was all the work of the mighty hands of God! When it's your time, it's your time and NOBODY can stop the plans God has for your life! Chadwick's death was a reminder that life was indeed fleeting. However, no matter how many bricks life throws your way, you can still be impactful and find the power in you to fight, push through the pain, and exhibit excellence in all things.

I WAS DREADING my six-month follow-up. The first diagnostic mammogram of my left breast had been looming over my head since my surgery. The mammogram was scheduled on September 25, which was just a few days after my birthday. My doctor told me that for insurance reasons, I was only going to have the left breast checked. I would be due to have the right breast checked in November. It was just a two-month time frame, so I didn't understand why both couldn't just be done at the same time. Ugh! On that day as I pulled into the parking lot, my anxiety was off the charts. I did not want to walk back into this same building where I had surgery and get back into the machine where I had that godawful wire placement in my left breast.

I thought back to the bad experience with my first lymphedema patient. She had PTSD from her breast cancer treatment. She told me how lying on treatment tables made her feel as if she was back in machines getting scans. I finally knew exactly how she felt. I was taken back into the changing room, then to wait for the mammography tech to take me back. She took one set of pictures.

"I will show these to the radiologist and see what she says," the tech said. I was escorted back to the waiting room. I had to repeatedly say, "Jesus, Jesus, Jesus" to calm my nerves. I knew that my last pathology report showed that all the cancer had not been removed, so I was nervous. I prayed, "God, please let these tests show what needs to be shown." The mammography tech came back to get me.

"The radiologist wants me to take another set of pictures just to get a better look," she said.

I took a deep breath because I did not want to get back into that machine. It was very painful. My breast was still very tender and healing from surgery. I was taken back to the waiting room to wait for the results.

I was told that calcifications were seen in the breast in the areas of the incision but they most likely were related to the extensive scar tissue in the breast and did not appear suspicious in nature. Hallelujah! I breathed a huge sigh of relief. "Thank you, God!"

After it was all said and done, I sat in the parking garage and cried. I needed to release those emotions.

About a week later I had a follow-up appointment with my breast surgeon. We sat down and discussed the results of my diagnostic mammogram.

"So it looks like they just see scar tissue, but after surgery we didn't get clear margins," she said.

I responded, "I know what that pathology report said, but I also know what those mammogram results show at this moment and what God said."

I told her that I was taking daily communion for healing in addition to my hormone therapy medication as instructed. I was not about to let anyone overshadow the fact that God was healing my body. I believe in medicine, but I trust God more.

ON NOVEMBER 18, 2020, tragedy struck my family once again. I normally take the interstate on my way home from work, but that particular day my intuition was signaling strongly for me to take the back roads home. I've learned to trust my gut whenever I get those inclinations. As I was about ten minutes into my forty-five-minute commute, my mom called.

"Are you driving?" she asked.

"Yes, I just left work not long ago. What's wrong?"

I could hear the concern in her voice. She told me that my uncle, her brother-in-law, had passed away suddenly while he and my aunt were at the grocery store. I was in shock!

"Let me pull over," I said. I pulled into a grocery store parking lot to try to process the news. It was clear that my intuition was leading me to take the back way home as I would not have been able to pull over on the interstate. My uncle passed away suddenly from what was believed to be another heart attack. He survived prostate cancer treatment, but left this world from a heart attack! It seemed so cruel! Here we were again, experiencing loss and death around the holidays. My poor auntie. I couldn't even imagine how she felt going into the grocery store, leaving my uncle sitting in the car, then coming out of the store to find him gone forever. She had lost her soulmate. I was devastated when I got the news. He was a very close uncle because my sisters and I often spent the summers at their Decatur, Georgia, home. We used to also go on family vacations with them. He treated us like we were his children. I went straight to her house once I got the news. I offered as much support and consolation to my aunt and cousins as I could. It was heartbreaking to see my aunt lamenting in shock and disbelief. Due to the pandemic, we were unable to gather together for Thanksgiving, so each household in my family spent Thanksgiving separately. We did gather together in limited numbers for my uncle's funeral which was on November 28, 2020, the Saturday after Thanksgiving. It was all surreal.

Shortly after, I was scheduled to have another diagnostic mammogram on December 1, 2020, this time to focus on my right breast. My doctor also wanted to check my left breast again just to make sure there were no changes. Ironically, this was so close to the date of December 5, 2019, when I received my very first diagnostic mammogram that subsequently led to my breast cancer diagnosis. This time I was not as nervous, but I still dreaded that mammography machine. My right breast was normal and the left breast was still showing calcifications in the scar tissue, unchanged from the previous scan. Hallelujah, again! God truly is a healer, but you have to have faith, trust, and continue to believe!

On December 14, 2020, I received a text message around midday from my best friend and foundation secretary. She told me to call her when I was home from work and settled. As soon as I got home, I called her. She told me our foundation vice president passed away. There were no funeral services and she was cremated. I burst into tears. My VP was in the nursing home recovering from a craniotomy that she had to have as a result of breast cancer metastasizing to her brain. I could not go visit her due to COVID-19. She truly was a fighter. She battled breast cancer for the three to four years that I knew her. She was like a second mom to me and my inspiration for starting Champions Can! Now she was gone. I was still grieving the loss of my uncle, and now I had to add this heartbreak to the mix. I hate cancer!

December 31, 2020, finally arrived. It was the end of the year, and I was so glad the holidays were over. I didn't even bother putting up Christmas decorations because having to take them down was a trigger for me. It was this time last year that I had my huge emotional breakdown as I was taking down my Christmas decorations after being diagnosed with breast cancer. I was happy that I had made it through the year. It was a rough one indeed.

With that being said, I was grateful for the ups and downs, as I now had resiliency and strength that I didn't even know I had. I spent New Year's Eve with a special man I met back in September. Right before we met, I had made up in my mind that I had been through so much that dating would not be my focus. I was not at the best place in my life emotionally or financially. I was lonely and needed emotional support, so I ended up getting a beagle puppy named Obsydian Snoopy Champion. I thought, "It's just gonna be me and my dog."

My first date with this man was actually on my birthday. Even though we had just met, he made me feel special on my birthday and was a complete gentleman. The conversation was amazing. Straight out of the gate, he asked me what was the hardest thing I had to deal with in 2020. I told him, "Breast cancer."

He paused and stared at me for a minute.

"Did you have to have your breasts removed?" he asked.

"No," I answered. I proceeded to tell him about the surgeries that I had. He listened very attentively.

"So are you good now?" he asked.

"Yes," I said.

"Okay, then, that's all that matters." He said I was beautiful and strong. Wow! I just told this man about the most insecure part of myself, and he still treated me like a human being. He didn't try to end the date or anything. He didn't ghost me. He was a real grown man, that's for sure! Meeting him was definitely a bright spot in my 2020. I didn't know if he was Mr. Right, but I did know that he was Mr. Right Now, and I enjoyed the journey of getting to know him. At that time, I felt that he was serving the purpose of restoring my self-confidence in dating after breast cancer as well as keeping me from sinking into a deep depression by offering me companionship during what could have been a very difficult holiday season, overshadowed by the awful memories of being diagnosed with breast cancer a year before.

# Phase Three
## Life Lessons in Finding My Purpose

## 26

## Purpose Defined

WHAT IS PURPOSE? WHAT IS YOUR PURPOSE IN LIFE? What is the purpose of the moment we are currently in? What is the purpose of the people we encounter? What are the fears that prevent you from fulfilling your purpose?

Bishop T. D. Jakes appeared on an episode of *Oprah's Lifeclass*. He talks about purpose by advocating that one should not "confuse talent with purpose." Bishop Jakes further expresses that "being good at something doesn't mean it's your calling."[1] During one of his sermons, titled "Living on Purpose," he says, "You must understand that purpose is an underlying chemistry that makes you live your life. However, if you're in a situation where your talents aren't being used to the maximum, it could be beneficial in the long run. You may start out doing something

---

[1] T. D. Jakes, *Oprah's Lifeclass*, Season 2 Episode 103, "Bishop T. D. Jakes on Living with Purpose, Part 1," aired April 09, 2012, on Oprah Winfery Network, https://www.oprah.com/oprahs-lifeclass/bishop-td-jakes-on-living-with-purpose-part-1-video.

that was not 'the thing' that you were created to do. It may only be the thing that leads to the thing you were created to do. So don't stop at where you are as if it were the destination, when in fact in reality it may be the transportation that brings you into that thing you were created to do."[1]

Wow! I thought there was a lot of purposeful power in that paragraph. I began to further research about purpose. What is purpose according to the Bible?

In Isaiah 43:7, the Bible makes it clear that God created man and that He created him for His glory. Therefore, the ultimate purpose of man, according to the Bible, is simply to glorify God. A harder question to answer, perhaps, is what does it look like to glorify God? In Psalm 100:2–3, we're told to worship God with gladness and "know that the Lord is God. It is he who made us, and we are his; we are his people, the sheep of his pasture."[2] Part of what it looks like to glorify God is to acknowledge who God is (our Creator, for starters) and to praise and worship Him as such.

In a passage written by Joel Osteen titled "You Are Made For A Purpose," he states the following:

"Understanding why God put you here is one of the most important principles when it comes to discovering your unique purpose and calling in life. The reason is that knowing why you are here on earth helps you answer the question of why God has uniquely gifted you the way He has, and what He has called you to accomplish individually. There's nothing more exciting than to discover your purpose, your area of calling and really focus on it! Don't let the enemy tell you you've been forgotten or left out. God has not left anybody out. You have talents, you have abilities, you have natural strengths and you need to be aware of what they are and make sure that you're taking advantage of them and using them for His glory. There

---

[1] T. D. Jakes, *Oprah's Lifeclass*, "You Shouldn't Confuse Talent with Purpose, aired April 10, 2012, on Oprah Winfrey Network, https://youtu.be/vOUPHd9UztK.
[2] New International Version.

is something important that only you can accomplish for God!"[1]

In *The Purpose Driven Life*, Pastor Rick Warren equates purpose to our mission in life. Are the two synonymous? He writes:

> *Your mission has eternal significance. It will impact the eternal destiny of other people, so it's more important than any job, achievement, or goal you will reach during your life on earth.*
>
> *The consequences of your mission will last forever; the consequences of your job will not. Nothing else you do will ever matter as much as helping people establish an eternal relationship with God. This is why we must be urgent about our mission. Jesus said, "All of us must quickly carry out the tasks assigned us by the one who sent me, because there is little time left before the night falls and all work comes to an end."*[2]

There are several Bible verses regarding purpose that I find insightful. Romans 8:28 reads, "And we know that all things work together for good to them that love God, to them who are the called according to his purpose."[3] Romans 12:6 tells us, "We have different gifts, according to the grace given to each of us."[4] We learn that God's purpose can't be undone, as Job 42:2 explains: "I know that you can do all things; no purpose of yours can be thwarted."[5]

Further into my search about purpose, I came across the idea of purpose as it relates to the celebration of Kwanzaa. Kwanzaa is a Swahili term that means "first fruits of the harvest." The holiday

---

[1] Joel Osteen, "Joel Osteen Daily Devotional Today's Word Jan 03 2018," JoelOsteen.life, January 3, 2018, http://joelosteen.life/joel-osteen-daily-devotional/joel-osteen-daily-devotional-jan-03-2018.html.
[2] Rick Warren, *The Purpose Driven Life* (Grand Rapids, MI: Zondervan, 2002), 284.
[3] King James Version.
[4] New International Version.
[5] New International Version.

is centered around seven principles of African heritage. Nia (Purpose) is one of the seven principles of Kwanzaa which means: "To make our collective vocation the building and developing of our community in order to restore our people to their traditional greatness."[1] I asked myself the following question: Is my purpose giving of the first fruits of my labor? Proverbs 3:9 says, "Honor the LORD with your wealth and with the best part of everything you produce."[2] My takeaway from this is while using my talents as a medical professional, I should always put my best effort forward while making it pleasing to God for the betterment and healing of mankind. According to Anna Sayce, the following are good questions to consider when trying to discover your life's purpose:

- What are some things you are passionate about in your life?
- What do you love doing?
- What do you want to bring to the lives of others?
- Do you feel happy and fulfilled with the career or life you currently have?
- What's blocking you from pursuing your true passion?[3]

If you don't know the answers to these questions yet, it is okay. I had to start trying to answer these questions, but I did not allow myself to become frustrated. I learned to give myself some grace to figure it out in my own time. I also had to look deep within myself while thinking about who I really was and what I really wanted out of life. Are you truly accepting of who you are as a person and the life experiences that have shaped your character today? Think of it this way: Anna Sayce also writes:

---

[1] "Kwanzaa," *Wikipedia.org*, https://en.wikipedia.org/wiki/Kwanzaa.
[2] New International Version.
[3] Anna Sayce, "How To Find Your Calling as a Lightworker," *Annasayce.com*, https://www.annasayce.com/how-to-find-your-calling-as-a-lightworker/.

*You can begin to attract the right calling on your life and discover your purpose when you know who you are, accept and value who you are, and are committed to being your true authentic self. Some of us are so far removed from our true selves and our values that over time, we have slowly begun to lose our inner moral compass which tells us what aligns with who we really are and what doesn't.*[1]

We end up ignoring our spirit and intuitive guidance and end up doing something just because others say we should or they think they know what we should be doing in life. Then we beat ourselves up with regret and wonder why we feel that we have no energy, motivation, or simply hate the career or life path that we are on. Trust me, I get it. I am definitely guilty of this.

On my journey to find my purpose, I had to learn some things the hard way. It is possible to be your authentic self, do what you love, and get paid for it. Follow your purpose and passion and the money will follow. This is by no means an easy feat, but don't be afraid to share your passion and gift with the world. Don't be afraid to chase after your passion. You never know who is watching and how many lives you are actually touching. That is another true definition of purpose.

I have often heard people say that the most unused potential is in a graveyard. Some people die without knowing their true purpose. There is no age limit to finding your purpose. Society has conditioned us to believe that we have to accomplish certain things in our life at a certain age. It does not always work like that. So what if you are fifty years old and you still don't know what your purpose is? What if you are seventy years old and still don't know? Each day you open your eyes is a new opportunity to seek out your purpose.

I always imagined I would be married with two kids and possibly halfway on another baby at my age. I never thought I would still be unmarried and childless at almost forty while also having to endure a breast cancer diagnosis. This was the hand I was dealt

---

[1] Ibid.

and I had to come to terms with it. It was all for a purpose. All in all, each stage in your life has a purpose and is not defined by the timelines society often imposes on us. God has a strategic timeline for your life and His purpose for your life cannot be undone. In other words, stop trying to keep up with the Joneses and just be you!

## 27

## Lightworking and Energy

I WAS RAISED A DEVOUT CHRISTIAN AND WAS TAUGHT that there is a fine line between the Bible, angels, spirits, lightworking, psychics, mediums, soothsayers, and New Age spiritual practices. Many people view these as forms of witchcraft. However, I began doing my own research. I frequently see number sequences on clocks, sometimes even on license plates. When it first started happening, I didn't think much of it. I said, "It's just a coincidence." However, it kept happening more and more frequently. Some of the common number sequences I saw—and still continue to see—include: 444, 923, 822, 911, 711, 555, 222, 333, 111, 1010, and 1111. After looking up the significance of these numbers, I discovered they were referred to as angel numbers. I began to find information about lightworking and receiving guidance from your angels as you perform your lightworking duties. Angel numbers are thought to give reassurance that you are on the right life path.

Hmmm . . . very interesting. What was this lightworking all about? As I researched more, I found that a lightworker is described as someone who is compassionate, empathetic, intuitive, a powerful manifestor, has the gift of receiving revelations in their dreams, frequently sees number sequences, highly awakened in regard to spiritual consciousness, and has the natural ability to heal and provide comfort to those around them physically, emotionally, and spiritually. These are all derived from Melanie Beckler, author and founder of www.Ask-Angels.com. (26)

These qualities all ring true for me and the experiences I have had in my life. I will provide some examples.

I THINK BACK to childhood as my mom always told me I had healing hands, even as a little girl. My patients also often tell me that they can feel my hands heating up as I am working on them. I always jokingly tell them "it is my healing power."

I have always had very vivid dreams that I often write down. At times, the dreams I have had have frightened me. I keep a journal in a drawer next to my bed so that I can write down my dreams as soon as I wake up. Much to my surprise, some of them have actually come true and I have been given a heads up for things that have happened in the future. I will never forget a dream I had that I had just gotten home from work and turned on the TV to the local news. I saw a yellow and red airplane landing in the middle of an interstate in Atlanta, however no one was hurt. I called my oldest sister and told her about the dream. "Sis, that is so crazy," she said. About a month or so later, I was watching the local news and lo and behold an airplane had made an emergency landing in the middle of I-85 in Atlanta and nobody was hurt. I called my sister again and said, "Sis, you won't believe what I just saw!" She was amazed and quickly recalled me telling her about a similar dream I had before I could even remind her about it. She always says, "Girl, your dreams scare me sometimes." Let's not forget about the dream I mentioned previously that I had in which I was riding through a storm on the back of a pickup truck during my breast cancer journey and came out of the storm unharmed. This was my revelation that I would be ok as I navigated my cancer journey.

A lightworker is also described as someone who shows others

how to overcome and recognize the blessings in obstacles and struggles as they walk their walk while inspiring lives in the process. I feel that my life is just that. No matter how many punches I take, I stay in the ring and keep fighting as an example to others that the only way you can stay down is if you want to stay down. I have been called a hero and a shero. I don't view myself in that way. I view myself as someone who tries to live my life as a positive example to others. It's not something I even feel that I am intentionally trying to do. It just happens. It is amazing how people have reached out to me to tell me how much I inspire them without me even realizing. It truly is a miraculous thing.

With continued research, I came across something called a Life Path Number, which is calculated using your birthday and is thought to give insight and information about your life's purpose. I did the math and found the number six to be my life path number. Numerologist Felicia Bender defines Life Path Six as a "nurturing visionary" and "champion of justice."[1] Afterall, my last name *is* Champion! People with this life path are also thought to be a lover of beauty, "goes against the grain" with regard to authority, yet often feel unappreciated, undervalued, and overwhelmed due to a lot of responsibilities thrown their way. Well, I did try to start a jewelry business. I have an "appreciate me or miss me" attitude, which is exactly how I felt when I left the hospital to start working for the neuropathy clinic that I hated. I also have a hard time understanding why others can't see the big picture the way that I can. A person with Life Path six can also be an "If you want something done right you just have to do it yourself" kind of person. This is me all day, every day! Learning how to accept help and delegating tasks to others is very hard for me, yet my breast cancer journey taught me that this is a character flaw that I need to work on in order to be the best version of myself. Life Path Six describes me perfectly. Reading about lightworking gave me greater insight into some of my personality characteristics as well as why I choose to do things a certain way. It also helped me realize why I have such

---

[1] Bender, Felicia. 6 Life Path: The Nurturing Visionary
https://feliciabender.com/six-life-path-2/

a strong inclination to want to try to take away everyone's pain and heal the world while being their "light" of hope and restoration.

Matthew 5:14-16 (KJV) says it best: "Ye are the light of the world. A city that is set on a hill cannot be hid. Neither do men light a candle, and put it under a bushel, but on a candlestick; and it giveth light unto all that are in the house. Let your light so shine before men, that they may see your good works, and glorify your Father which is in heaven."

With that being said, I will continue to shine on!

I VISITED NEW Orleans with a group of friends in July 2017. As we ventured down Decatur Street, an outdoor artist market caught my attention. We passed it and continued to check out other shops along the street. As we journeyed back to our hotel, we passed the market again. I was compelled to stop. Immediately upon entering, there was a woman who had a table set up with beautiful handmade pendant necklaces. One particular necklace caught my attention. It was a large amethyst stone wrapped in silver wire in a very unique design. I held it in my hand and admired it and placed it back on the table. I wanted to see what else was in the market, so I ventured off to explore. Nothing else seemed to be of interest to me. I was drawn back to the table with the beautiful pendants and immediately picked up the amethyst necklace. It was the most uniquely cut stone on the table. The designer said, "I watched you as you entered. Then you came back. You were initially drawn to this necklace. It is amazing how people are drawn sometimes to what they need." She told me that the amethyst stone had healing properties. I just wanted it for its beauty, so I purchased it. She placed the necklace around my neck and hugged me and I also agreed to let her take a picture of me wearing the necklace to place on her website. She had this positive aura about her that I could not put into words. She told me to go to her website to read about the amethyst stone. I found the following information posted alongside a picture of the pendant I purchased from her:

She described the stone as follows:

Amethyst is a powerful and protective stone. . . . Amethyst relieves stress and strain, soothes irritability, balances mood swings, dispels anger, rage, fear, and anxiety. It activates spiritual awareness, opens intuition, and enhances psychic abilities. It has strong healing and cleansing powers. Amethyst boosts hormone production, tunes the endocrine system and metabolism. It strengthens the immune system, reduces pain and strengthens the body to fight against cancer. It destroys malignant tumors and aids in tissue regeneration. It cleanses the blood and relieves physical, emotional and psychological pain or stress. Amethyst eases headaches and releases tension. It reduces bruising, swellings, injuries, and treats hearing disorders. Amethyst heals diseases of the lungs and respiratory tract, skin conditions, cellular disorders and diseases of the digestive tract.[1]

Hmmm . . . very interesting read! I was in awe as I read about the stone. Many of the healing properties of the stone lined up with what I felt that I needed at the time. I was stressed out, grieving the end of a relationship and being single again. I was having vivid dreams and questioning their meaning. I work with cancer patients, and, boy, do I have mood swings! She was right. I gravitated to that necklace because I needed it to help center and balance my energy at the time. A close friend introduced me to energy healing, and I decided to go visit an energy healer. During my first encounter with her, I was quite skeptical because she operated her business out of her home basement. To my surprise, she lived less than two miles from my house. Upon entering her basement, I felt a sense of calm from the sweet aroma of incense. I was surprised when I saw her. She was a very petite woman from Indonesia, very mild-mannered and soft-spoken. She took me into a room with a treatment table and a couch. It was dimly

---

[1] Asta Levine, "Amethyst-Purple," Triple Eight Jewelry, https://www.facebook.com/permalink.php?id=869791239730131&story _fbid=3468774633165099.

lit. As I sat down on the couch, I again felt a sense of calm. Truthfully, the atmosphere was so soothing that it made me want to go to sleep. She asked me about things that were going on in my life. I immediately opened up to her and expressed my true feelings. Normally, people rely on me for advice and answers and come to me with their problems, so it was like a huge exhale for me to be able to talk to her about my concerns, feelings, desires, and dreams. Unbeknownst to me, my energy healer was also a clairvoyant. She spoke to me about things that were happening in my life that I had not yet told her. She revealed to me that I had a lot of angels and "spirit guides" around me that were always supporting and protecting me. That explained and confirmed for me the strange series of numbers I constantly saw. She also revealed that I had a very strong third eye, wisdom, and insight and that I should see what lessons there are for me to learn in the vivid dreams that I have frequently. She picked up on the fact that I worked in a healing profession and saw that an older female with short hair had an attachment to me. This was an interesting acknowledgment because I was currently working with a breast cancer survivor, treating her for lymphedema. The patient was very emotional, had high anxiety, and was indeed very attached to me. I never told my energy healer what my profession was, yet she already knew. She also told me that I have a strong prayer connection with God and that when I pray, He definitely listens to me and I capture the attention of my spirit guides.

My energy healer taught me the importance of setting boundaries and not taking on everyone's negative energy and problems, as it was depleting my energy. Before starting my day, she instructed me to imagine myself being surrounded by a protective light and not allowing anyone to penetrate that light as I went about my day. At the end of the day, she instructed me to say, "I release all negative attachments I encountered today." Even now I protect my energy at all costs. I believe that positive energy produces a purposeful position.

## 28

## Confirmation and Inner Promptings of the Spirit

I HAVE ALWAYS HAD STRONG INTUITION, AND I HAVE learned over the years to really listen to my intuition for guidance.

I had a strong inner voice telling me to go to church on a Sunday in July 2017, particularly the 7:30 a.m. service. I obliged and gathered my clothing together the night before. I woke up early Sunday before my alarm went off, got dressed, and went to church as planned. As they did altar call, I stood at my seat and prayed silently for myself and my family, and my profession.

As church was dismissed, one of the female ministers stopped me and asked, "Can I talk to you for a minute?"

"Sure!" I said.

"I kept staring and staring at you, and I don't know why the spirit kept telling me to come to you and pray for you," she said. "But I could not leave here without being obedient to the spirit." She asked if she could pray with me.

We held hands and she began to pray. The tears started to flow as she prayed about everything that I had been deeply thinking about.

"I see God in her," she said. "She will touch the lives of many. Everyone that she touches will be healed. I pray that she comes into contact with the right people at the right time and talks to who she needs to talk to, to take her to the next level." She also prayed over my family, finances, and career. It was definitely confirmation!

ON APRIL 1, 2018, I returned to White Plains to visit my parents for Easter. We had such a great time that I left home a little later than I normally would to head back to Atlanta, which was around 7:15 p.m. My navigation app gave me the all-clear to take I-20 Westbound as I normally do. About thirty to forty minutes into my trip, traffic came to a COMPLETE standstill. The GPS still said traffic was clear. After sitting for thirty minutes, the app updated and stated it was a two-hour delay due to a major crash. I called my middle sister because I knew she had already left my parents' house and was heading up I-20 Westbound to Conyers. Luckily, I caught her in time to reroute her off of another exit. She avoided being stuck and made it home in about an hour.

Other cars in certain areas were turning around in the median. However, where I was sitting, the median was too deep for me to attempt to turn around and I would have gotten stuck. So, I waited and waited and waited but only moved maybe a half-mile in two hours. The next exit was still three miles away and nobody was moving. The cellular network was clogged up, so I couldn't even call my family and I couldn't access my GPS to try to reroute around the traffic mess.

After hours of sitting and creeping what seemed like five feet every so often, I finally moved to a point at which I could cross the median to the eastbound lanes and turn around. After getting out of the traffic jam, my cellular data kicked back in and I was able to use my GPS. It was 11:00 p.m. at night, and I was rerouted through extremely dark, windy, and unfamiliar backroads to get home. Exhausted and frustrated, I turned on Joel Osteen and kept it pushing. Ironically, his message was about divine interruptions.

My goal was to get home and get home safely. By midnight, I had finally made it home. My family was relieved. I didn't get home in the time I anticipated or on the route anticipated, but I made it!

This whole situation taught me several things:

> Lesson 1: If I had left my parents' house thirty minutes earlier, it could have been me in that fatal wreck and the conversation would be totally different right now.
>
> Lesson 2: We all have goals in life that we want to accomplish. Sometimes God will cause a delay and you have to wait and wait and wait until, finally, the time is right to make a move. Sometimes other people will accomplish their goal faster than you. You may be taken on an alternate route and sometimes the route may be dark with winding roads, and you will be frustrated, tired, and exhausted along the way. However, God will get you where you want to be to accomplish your goal in His time! It may not be done in the time you wanted, or may not happen the way you thought it would happen, or there will be curves and alternate routes along the way, but it will happen! Be patient and stay consistent and accept the delays as blessings!

I hope this will bless you!

One thing I do know is that "God goes before me and makes my crooked paths straight," regardless of the detours we take in life.[1]

---

[1] Isaiah 45:2 (New International Version).

## 29

## My Inspirational Influence on Others

SOMETIMES WE GET SO CAUGHT UP IN THE INNER workings and busyness of our everyday lives that we forget the level of impact that we have on people that we encounter. This letter I received from a dear friend and patient reminded me of this. The letter reads as follows:

> *A Crystal is a precious gemstone. You are an individual precious gem, a gift from God. You cannot imagine how thankful I am that the Lord brought you into my life. Crystals are used to manifest health and happiness. Crystal healing therapy involves placing gemstones on the body or underneath pillows to ward off sickness, draw out negative energy, and absorb positive energy. Crystal healing is an alternative medical technique in which crystals and other stones are used to cure ailments and protect against disease.*
>
> *The name Crystal is a variant of Christian, a follower of Christ. It is plain to see that Christ lives in you. You*

*exude health, happiness, and positivity in all that you say and do.*

*The name Ann derives from the ancient Greek form of the Hebrew names Anna and Hanna, eating grace or gracious. Your hands are healing, your heart is warm, and your spirit is gracious.*

*A Champion is exactly what you are. A Champion is a person who fights or argues for a cause on behalf of someone else. A Champion is also defined as an advocate, proponent, promoter, supporter, defender, upholder, and backer. Champion is also a verb that means to support the cause of, or defend.*

*On behalf of all lymphedema patients, thank you for being our Champion. I firmly believe that God chose you to share your gifts, your wisdom, and your knowledge to initiate this much needed program that helps so many people. I am grateful to be among those who benefit from your skills and expertise. Thank you for going the extra mile, above and beyond, to provide the treatment, therapy, services, and supplies that we all so desperately need.*

*I want you to know how much I appreciate you. Not only have you helped me physically, but you have also helped me emotionally. Everything you say, and how you say it, makes a difference in my day. I hope you know now, and will always know, that in a short amount of time, you have added to my life in immeasurable ways. I cannot thank you enough.*

*It is evident that you chose this career path because you have a passion for helping people get better and continue to be better. You are caring, kind, considerate, and thoughtful. Thank you for allowing God to use you as a vessel to bless me and so many others. You are everything mentioned above and so much more. I am honored to call you my doctor, my therapist, and my friend. May God's richest blessings be yours today and always.*

*Love Always,*
*Your Patient and Friend*

My oldest sister always calls me her greatest inspiration, even though I'm eight years younger than she is. One day she made a social media post on what was recognized as National Siblings Day.

A letter to my sister:

> *Dear Crystal,*
>
> *I just want you to know that I am beyond blessed to have you as my sister. We have shared a bond and friendship that is unbreakable. I know that we have had our differences and fallouts from time to time, but we have always managed to work through them quickly. It is funny that when we do have our little falling outs, we would call one or the other to find out if we have heard from each other, LOL! I love you more than words can ever express.*
>
> *Cook, I will always say that we are twins born eight years apart. Baby sister, I am so proud of the woman that you are and continue to become. I admire you because you are a go-getter. Whatever you set your mind to God gives you the strength and fortitude to always accomplish those things that you pursue. I admire you for your courage and strength. Fearless is the word that perfectly describes you. You don't mind hopping on a plane and traveling all around the world by your damn self, while dad is at home having a conniption because he doesn't have a passport to go and get you, LOL! I admire you for your brilliant mind and sensibility. I admire you for your no-nonsense demeanor. You will cut a person down quick if they come at you wrong.*
>
> *I say all of this to say that I love you dearly. You always see the potential and abilities that I have that I oftentimes do not see in myself. You are my God given cheerleader. I appreciate you more than you all could ever know. I know that I haven't been the perfect older sister or set the best examples, but I hope that I have made you proud of me just as I am proud of you.*
>
> *Love always and forever,*<br>*Your Oldest Sister.*

My sister was right. I was fearless. I was so fearless that I actually went skydiving for my thirty-seventh birthday. It was a bucket list item. I went with a group of friends. The weather was absolutely gorgeous with sunny clear blue skies. We had a perfect view of the other people skydiving. The anticipation was building. Once I was suited up and on the plane, it was the point of no return. My instructor hooked himself to the back of me. The door of the plane opened, and my instructor and I scooted closer to the open door.

"Oh my God, I'm really about to do this!" I said.

He told me to place my feet on the edge of the door and tilt my head back. He counted, "One, two, three!" We leaped out of the plane, somersaulted, and then free-fell for twelve to fourteen seconds before our parachute opened. Thank God the parachute opened! It was the most liberating feeling ever! My instructor let me steer the parachute around in a circle. The view was amazing. Then we landed. I couldn't believe I actually did it! I recalled a quote that said, "God places the best things on the other side of fear." Surely if I could conquer skydiving, I could conquer anything else that came my way.

I didn't tell my sisters or parents about my skydiving excursion until after I had done it. My dad had a fit!

"You did what?" he said. "You mean to tell me you jumped out of a perfectly good plane? Lord have mercy! If God wanted you to fly, He would have given you wings and if He wanted you to swim, He would have given you fins. Stay out of the water and stay out of the air!"

My mom was calm, cool, and collected. After my dad was done ranting and raving, she chimed in and said, "Well, did you have fun?"

"Yep!" I answered.

"Well, that's all that matters!"

I actually sprained my right foot and ankle on the landing and had to wear a walking boot for six weeks, but the experience was worth it. I printed out a picture of myself skydiving and placed it in my treatment room for my cancer patients to know that they, too, could conquer their fear of cancer.

IN EARLY FEBRUARY 2020, my friend and I were in the process of searching for a venue to have our next Survivorship Day party for my nonprofit. My friend stumbled upon a hidden gem of a wedding venue outside of Atlanta. The venue was having an open house event and we were invited to attend free of charge to check out the venue to see it if would be suitable for our needs. We were able to have a one-on-one sit-down with the owner. He wanted to know more about our foundation. I gave him a folder of information about the foundation in addition to the survivorship guide I had written. I told him that the entire board was comprised of breast cancer survivors and that I had also been recently diagnosed. He told us that he had a friend who died of cancer who also wanted to do nonprofit work to help cancer survivors, so he felt that he had a duty to continue to help his friend carry out this mission. To our surprise, he also said that he was a certified public accountant (CPA) and had just purchased an auction company. His goal was to be able to take several charities under his wing to help develop them and help their fundraising to make a larger impact. Wow! This man didn't know us from a can of paint and wanted to help us. He was exactly what we needed to help take the foundation to a whole new level! He was definitely a divine connection and a blessing from God!

I RECEIVED A RANDOM PHONE CALL OCTOBER 2, 2020, from a woman who was looking to donate her handmade jewelry to a nonprofit foundation. She told me she had bracelets made that had a cancer ribbon charm on them. The phone call caught me off guard, but I was grateful to accept the bracelets, especially with it being Breast Cancer Awareness Month. We arranged a day and time to meet up at a local park because we both lived in the same city. She also told me that I was the only person that answered the phone after she had attempted to call other organizations in the area. Once we met up, we stood and talked in the parking lot for at least forty-five minutes! It was like we were two good girlfriends who had known each other forever! Not to mention the bracelets she donated were beautiful. She told me that she had a passion for writing and had previously written a book. I told her that I was working on a book and needed help with organization and structure. It was put in my spirit to ask, "Have you ever thought about starting your own book publishing company?" Her face lit up and I got goosebumps all over as I told her. She told me she was going to go for it. In less than a month, she sent me a screenshot of her articles of incorporation for her publishing company! Once again, I believe she was a divine connection. It was no coincidence that I was the only organization that answered her phone call. We crossed paths to inspire each other. I've learned over the years to always evaluate who crosses your path and why. Never overlook the opportunity to uplift someone else, even when you are going through your own trials and difficult times in life. This is when your real blessings come. Always be open to divine connections!

## 30

## The Point and Purpose of It All

SO NOW HERE I AM, SHARING MY LIFE STORY WITH you. The good, the bad, the ugly, the painful, the real, the raw. Why am I writing this book? Why am I sharing my story? Why am I bearing my soul and life to the world? What do I really want people to know? What am I really trying to say? What I do know is that my truths are my truths. My life experiences have taught me the following:

- I am too hard on myself. It's okay to chill and do nothing sometimes. Normalize not feeling guilty for taking the breaks that you deserve to recharge your batteries.
- You cannot pour from an empty cup.
- It doesn't matter if the glass is half empty or half full; what matters is that there is something in it, which means you still have a life to live and a purpose to fulfill.

- You have to sometimes release something to gain something. You can't expect to get something new if you are still holding on to garbage, things that have expired, and things that no longer positively serve you.
- It's okay for me to say NO without an explanation and have no regrets about it. Boundaries are essential to your peace and well-being.
- It's okay to outgrow people. Some people are seasonal.
- Always remain teachable and willing to learn. Everybody can always learn something new from someone else.
- Not everyone will understand my vision. I can't be a giraffe grazing in the trees and expect a turtle moving sluggishly across the terrain to understand ALL OF ME!
- I have a very low tolerance for BS, ignorance, immaturity, and beating around the bush. Say what you mean and mean what you say!
- I love the brown skin I am in more than I ever have: natural hair, stretch marks, cellulite, love handles, and all!
- I am fearless! Skydiving proved that!
- I am much stronger than I thought I was. God gives you a load to carry based on your foundation and infrastructure. He will never put more on you than you can handle.
- I have a greater respect for differences between people. Everybody needs healing, regardless of the color of their skin.
- I discovered my own spiritual journey that is in alignment with my soul and life purpose.
- Time is not promised or guaranteed to anyone. I am on God's timetable, not anyone else's or where they think I should be in my life.

- Always move in silence. Keep negative energy away from your goals and dreams. Not everyone wants to see you win!
- I am loved and capable of receiving love.
- Don't expect out of other people what I expect of myself. Be more gracious with people who are much different than me.
- When the flames start, not everyone who you thought would help you will be there to cool you off. Ghosting is real!
- It's okay to not be okay. There is beauty in vulnerability.
- Being smart is more popular than being popular.
- I don't have to wear the "strong, independent woman" cape 24/7. It's okay to accept help.
- Don't ever tell someone you know how they feel if you have not personally been through it.
- God's "NO" doesn't mean it will never happen, it just means not right now.
- I am exactly where I am supposed to be. Everything is divinely orchestrated, down to the millisecond!
- Let everything you do be done with purpose and intent.
- Always remain humble. Your entire life can be changed in an instant.
- Do what you love and are passionate about and your material needs will always be met.
- Last but not least, my life is not all about me . . . It's about Christ working through me so that I may serve others. That's the ultimate legacy I wish to imprint upon this earth.

THE WEEK OF April 10, 2016, it was placed in my spirit while I sat in church to write a book and share the story of how God has allowed certain events to unfold in my life. A guest minister spoke in church that day. Her topic was "Take It to Jesus." Her

Biblical reference was Luke 13:10–16 which highlighted the story of how Jesus healed a woman on the Sabbath who was crippled for eighteen years by an evil spirit and walked bent over. The minister posed the following question: "What in your life is crippling you?"

Hmmm. I sat there, reflecting, thinking, and taking it all in.

She said, "Whatever is crippling you, you have been set free!"

Jesus told the crippled woman in Verse 12 of the same passage, "Woman, thou art loosed from thine infirmity."[1]

I realized I was being set free from doubt, fear of the unknown, fear of failure, the opinions of others, the scrutiny of others, and even my own insecurities. I began to reflect on my life. It was revealed to me: share your story of how God has blessed you, spoken to you, unleashed his abundant favor in your life, and how you are ultimately at peace as you are walking in your purpose. At the end of the day, God's message to me was "Do what I ask you to do, even small things, focus on helping my people, follow your passion for helping cancer patients and survivors, and I will continue to align you with the right people at the right time." I always believed if you take that first step of faith, God will take ten thousand more for you. Things were not unfolding the way I had planned, but they were unfolding according to God's timing, His calibration of my life, and His ultimate plan for me. We often have misconceptions about faith, religion, God, and what it all means. To me, religion and faith are all about using your life to help others. We were all put here on this Earth for a purpose. There are so many unanswered questions: Who created the earth? Are we the only humans in the universe? What is space and the infinite amount of black space and planets beyond our own? Who is God? What is God? Are we all on different paths that ultimately lead us to the same goal, the same God, an entity that cannot be quantified or put into words?

NEW YEAR'S DAY 2021 was a cold, cloudy, and rainy day. The rain was torrential at times. As I was laying in bed, I

---

[1] King James Bible.

began reflecting on my life up until my current circumstances. I was scrolling online and came across the following passage:

> Your calling is going to crush you. If you are called to mend the broken-hearted, you're going to wrestle with broken-heartedness. If you are called to prophesy, you're going to struggle to control your mouth. If you are called to lay hands, you're going to struggle with spiritual viruses. If you are called to preach and teach the gospel, you will be sifted for the wisdom that anoints your message. If you are called to empower, your self-esteem will be attacked, your successes will be hard-fought. Your calling will come with cups, thorns, and sifting that are necessary for your mantle to be authentic humble, and powerful. Your crushing won't be easy because your assignment is not easy. Your oil is not cheap.[1]

That was it! If I was called to restore hope to those with cancer and lymphedema, I had to endure a cancer diagnosis and all of the physical, emotional, and financial strain that came along with it. I recall in the days leading up to my diagnosis, I was listening to my favorite pastor, Joel Osteen, as I normally did when I was driving. In his messages that particular week, I kept feeling I was being prepared for something, but did not yet know what it was. His message touched on battling health issues and unexpected bad breaks. Deep down in my spirit, I knew I needed to walk the cancer journey to be able to have a larger impact on people as I fulfilled my purpose. I was in a much different place at the start of 2021 than I was this time last year. As 2021 came to a start, everything had now seemed to come full circle. It was a rainy day. The rain to me was symbolic of 2020 being washed away. The vision was clear. The year 2020 was a year of self-reflection, clarity,

---

[1] I traced the source of this quote to a sermon titled "Your Oil Is Not Cheap" by Pastor Patrick Weaver at Faithhill Church in San Leandro, California, though the specific source was difficult to find.

revelation, and faith. I vowed that 2021 was going to be a year of restoration and recovery. Yes, I had a lot of losses, but I knew I still had much more to gain.

So, who is Crystal Ann Champion, Dr. Champion, Bubbles, Cook, Cookie, Cookie Monster, Cookster, Cristal (like the Champagne), the physical therapist, the simple country Black girl with a passion and a dream? I am often told I am difficult to read, smart, witty, intelligent, ambitious, insightful, free-spirited, well-cultured, well-traveled, a go-getter, uptight, type-A, a motivator, someone who inspires, someone who is fearless, blunt, straight to the point, determined, family-oriented, caring, successful, strong-willed, and a perfectionist. I do know that I am all that God created me to be, and without Him I am nothing. God has defined me as a unique "cookie in the jar," a woman of valor, a woman of favor, a virtuous woman, a courageous woman, a fearless woman who has an assignment that no one else on this Earth has: to help others in only the way I know how which is more than enough to leave a lasting impression on and a legacy for His people. God is not nearly finished writing my story, but through His grace and mercy, I am allowed to continue to walk into my purpose. After all, my life is not my own.

# Gallery

Baby Picture

Kindergarten

Marching Band

College Graduation

My Private Practice,
Eminence Physical Therapy

My nonprofit organization,
Champions Can! Foundation
for Cancer Wellness, Inc.

Living Beyond Breast Cancer Conference (Pre-Breast Cancer Diagnosis)

The Network Journal "40 Under Forty" Awards Ceremony October 2019

At the fundraising event I attended the day I was diagnosed with breast cancer December 31, 2019

The "God Is Dope" van I saw on my way home after I picked up my medical reports from the breast imaging center

Breast Cancer Surgery Day
February 18, 2020

Recovering after breast surgery

Birthday Celebration During the COVID-19 Pandemic and Protests

Skydiving

# Bibliography

Bender, Felicia. 6 Life Path: The Nurturing Visionary https://feliciabender.com/six-life-path-2/

Jakes, T. D. *Oprah's Lifeclass*. Season 2, episode 103. "Bishop T. D. Jakes on Living with Purpose, Part 1." Aired April 09, 2012. Oprah Winfrey Network. https://www.oprah.com/oprahs-lifeclass/bishop-td-jakes-on-living-with-purpose-part-1-video.

Jakes, T. D. *Oprah's Lifeclass*. "You Shouldn't Confuse Talent with Purpose. Aired April 10, 2012. Oprah Winfrey Network. https://youtu.be/vOUPHd9UztK.

"Kwanzaa." *Wikipedia.org*. https://en.wikipedia.org/wiki/Kwanzaa.

Levine, Asta. "Amethyst-Purple." Triple Eight Jewelry. https://www.facebook.com/permalink.php?id=869791239730131&story_fbid=3468774633165099.

Sayce, Anna. "How To Find Your Calling as a Lightworker." *Annasayce.com*. https://www.annasayce.com/how-to-find-your-calling-as-a-lightworker/.

Warren, Rick. *The Purpose Driven Life: What on Earth Am I Here For?* Grand Rapids, MI: Zondervan, 2002.

Woods, Candace B. *While I Wait: An Inspirational Guide for Single and Divorced Women in Their Season of Waiting.* 2016.

# About the Author

Dr. Crystal A. Champion is a speaker, author, and entrepreneur. She is a physical therapist specializing in cancer rehabilitation and lymphedema treatment. She is also a breast cancer survivor. She is the founder of the nonprofit organization, Champions Can! Foundation for Cancer Wellness, Inc. that supports and advocates for cancer survivors and their families.

CPSIA information can be obtained
at www.ICGtesting.com
Printed in the USA
LVHW011543201122
733651LV00002B/228

9 781665 302029